Harvest Creek
PUBLISHING

Cry of My *Heart*

Meditations & Prayers for Adoptive Moms

BETH ANNE NAGEL

Teresa Granberry/Harvest Creek Publishing
10891 Dauphine
Willis, Texas 77318
www.harvestcreek.net

Cover and Book Layout © 2020 Harvest Creek Design

Ordering Information:
Quantity sales. Special discounts are available on quantity purchases by corporations, associations, and others. For details, please contact Beth Nagel

Cry of My Heart/Beth Nagel. –1ˢᵗ ed.
ISBN 978-0-578-67898-6

DEDICATION

For my husband, Rich: You believed God could
minister to others through my writing, long before
anyone else.

For my children: You inspire me to keep
my eyes on Jesus.

For my tribe of Trauma Mommas: Our Thursday night
Coffee Club helps me remember that I am not
the "bad guy."

ACKNOWLEDGMENTS

ADOPTION IS beautiful and wonderful, and it is also ugly and awful. Every adoptive family has a unique story. Some families sail through life after adoption without a single battle against trauma. If that is you, consider yourself blessed and read these pages to better understand the struggles some of us are walking through.

Parenting kids who have come from difficult beginnings can be exhausting. It is difficult for us to know why they can't just let something go. After all, we love them, protect them, feed them, and pray for them. This therapeutic approach to parenting that we try to navigate can also be inexplicably rewarding whenever you see your child experience even a glimpse or taste of real peace.

I am so grateful for El-Roi, the God who sees. He knew this book would be written long before I even knew I would write it. The words that have flowed through my typing fingers came from Him; I have no doubt. All I ask of him is that he will use this work to minister to the hearts of whomever he pleases.

I also will not hesitate to thank my husband, Rich. Babe, you are everything I asked God to bring me and then some. You have never left me thinking that I am entirely alone on this path that is laid out. You have sent me shopping when you sensed I need a break (*even though I have a strong dislike for any kind of shopping*). You support my running habit even though running shoes are not cheap, and training for a race means time away from home. You also believed I was a writer before I did. You are my logic when I am not thinking clearly. You are, without a doubt, my match made in heaven. Thank you.

I would be remiss in not mentioning my children. The stories in these pages are not just mine. They are also yours. You are the ones who spent the beginnings of life in fear and uncertainty. Thank you for permitting me to share our experience with other families who may be struggling. You have survived what many will never even have to consider. You are each amazing, brilliant, compassionate followers of Jesus. Thank you for the opportunity to be your mom even on the days when I am not very likable or *mom*-ish. I am honored each time you can choose to let me in; I know it is hard.

My tribe of Trauma Mommas, Carrie, Kim, Kristen, Pam, you lovers of Jesus and his little ones, serve me well each time I reach out. God holds each of our families in his loving hands, and it is so much easier to rest in that—with you at my side. You climb down into the pit with me and usually make me laugh until I wet myself.

Angie, how you put up with me for a sister for 45 years is a miracle in itself. I am incredibly grateful for your support, prayers, and excitement for this project.

My kids have a connection with their Auntie and Uncle that they will always be able to cherish.

Virginia, my long-distance bestie, you may not have adopted children, but you sure do know how to seek the Lord on my behalf when all the text message says is, "I'm not okay." Now, if we can just get our husbands to see fit to locate us in the same state!

DeAnn, my long-time ministry friend, thanks for providing your excellent photography skills to capture the perfect shot for my author photo.

Cindy, my virtual big sis, thank you for connecting me with Teresa. I am confident **Cry of my Heart** would not be more than scribbles on a journal page otherwise.

To all that I have failed to mention, you know who you are, and God knows who you are. Thank you for letting him use you to bolster me.

CONTENTS

FOREWORD

AS A YOUNG PASTOR, I wondered week after week about the constant struggle of a teenage girl from a devout Christian family. What was God up to? This young lady sought God at an altar of prayer, wrestling with the enemy of her soul, more times than I can count. The saints of God would faithfully gather around her until she was through with the present struggle and repeat the scene as necessary to see this child of God be victorious. This young lady grew into a woman of God with a heart for the hurting.

While serving as her pastor, I also worked as a social worker with children and families in crisis, investigating allegations of child abuse and neglect. I helped children and families caught in the juvenile justice system and assisted children moving in and through the adoption process when efforts for rehabilitation and reunification had failed—watching children of trauma become adult children of trauma and then the cycle repeats.

Little did I know that after nearly 30 years in this work, the path of that teenage girl, struggling to hold onto God and find His purpose, and my path would cross again through her efforts to raise children of trauma, for whom God gave her a heart, and made her their Momma through adoption.

Once again, through the pages of this book, her heart for God shines through. She is continually seeking His grace, His strength, and His wisdom to be able to pour into these precious lives the worth, love, and value with which God sees them. When living with and raising children who have experienced early childhood trauma, the stress is sometimes more than one might think they can bear.

But out of that beautiful struggle comes the cry of the heart. That cry can sometimes be voiced, but often it is something only the Spirit can understand and take before the throne of God with groaning that cannot be uttered (Romans 8:26).

Through the pages of this book, Beth has recorded prayers and scriptures for wisdom, strength, and grace, in the hope of encouraging others who are walking this path. But between the lines lies the struggle, pain, and the question of "How can I do this, Lord?" It is here, between the lines where lies the Cry of My Heart!

Pastor Charles Davenport, MA
Permanency Resource Monitor
State of Michigan

INTRODUCTION

They had sought him with all their heart, and he was found by them. So, the LORD gave them rest on every side.
−2 Chronicles 15:15b

IN THE VERY EARLY STAGES of **Cry of My Heart**, I had two primary goals: 1) get these meditations and prayers into the hands of as many adoptive moms as possible and 2) ensure that the opportunities for reflection were brief enough to receive truth for the day without requiring great lengths of time. Therapeutic parenting is not something for which a person should seek a final arrival, but rather a sacred call to lay aside human insufficiency and submit to God's all-sufficiency.

It's an invitation to develop a walk with God worth imitating. You will find within these pages not just recommendations for parenting kids from hard beginnings, you will find a new perspective on your kids, yourself, and your role as a Trauma Momma. Mostly I pray that you will find assurance for mothering each day.

Each of the 52 Meditations begins with a title and passage of scripture to set the tone. There will be a brief narrative drawn from the collection of my own challenges, joys, and struggles as an adoptive mom. The Meditations with a ♥ in the title are ideas that came directly from my children when I asked what they would write to adoptive families. After each narrative, you will have the opportunity to reflect with me on the possible takeaway from the story.

An invitation to agree with me in prayer follows. You most absolutely can change this prayer in any way that you desire to fit your unique circumstances.

When you are ready, take the time to use the lines provided to etch out the cries of your own heart. Or, perhaps, you would prefer to invite the Holy Spirit to carry the cries of your heart to God while you ask God to provide you with a word or phrase that you can easily meditate on throughout the day or week.

Do all of this as little or as often as you like. You may find that some days you only have the wherewithal to glance at the prayer for a nugget of hope. Others of you may choose one meditation to read and re-read every day and reiterate your heart's cry or call out an entirely new one.

Most of all, invite the Lord to direct your time. After all, he knows better than we do what we need.

PREFACE

He who calls you is faithful; he will do it."
−1 Thessalonians 5:24

DANDELIONS have always held a special place in my heart. I have fond memories of collecting them by the bucketful, so my momma could make a batch of delightful yellow jelly that was bright as the sunshine and as sweet as, well, jelly. Sometimes my sister and I would collect big bunches and deliver them to our momma as a bouquet in a water glass. Momma always feigned pleasure and surprise over our gift even when the pickings were slim and the flowers more brown than yellow.

The part about dandelions I have never understood is that they are considered *weeds*. Though they are as bold and beautiful as a field of sunflowers, folks spend a lot of time and money to eradicate them. Once, our neighbor scolded my dad for allowing me to pick dandelions that had gone to seed, as I gently blew them into the wind. There's nothing quite as peaceful as watching those tiny poofs float through the sun's rays on a path toward a new home (*likely in the neighbor's yard*).

When I think about dandelions today, I still look forward to the beauty in a golden carpet that unfurls across our field. Just like when I was a little girl, I love to watch the sun glisten through the seeds, making them altogether a heavenly sight. It seems rare for me to find a kindred spirit regarding dandelions, but I figure God thinks they are beautiful, so *his* Spirit can be *my* kindred spirit. I'm okay with that.

Adoption is a lot like a dandelion. Depending on your perspective, the unique disposition of an adoptive family may be beautiful, ugly, wonderful, awful, lovely, out-of-control, memorable, falling apart, or even *all* of the above. Every story is different, and every story is the same.

Adoption stories differ in that each child comes to your home with unparalleled early life experiences. Adoption stories are the same in that as research shows, when a child is removed from their primary attachment, e.g., biological mother, it impedes that child's mental, emotional, and even physical development. The more traumatic the separation, the more negative the developmental ramifications.

Cry of my Heart was born out of my desperate plea to the Father for answers. As I navigated the world of adoption, connected with adoptive moms, and heard their stories, my sense of helplessness only increased. Sharing my heartache with my husband, I said, "This just isn't right. We are surrounded by adoptive families who are falling apart at the seams because there is little understanding or support available. I don't know what to do, but I sense that I'm supposed to do something."

Recruiting a precious sister in Christ, we committed to pray every day for a month and share what God revealed. At the end of the 31 days, the only thing either of us reported was, "Pray." So that's exactly what I did!

Writing down prayers that flowed out of my heart, and sharing them with other adoptive moms, became a sort of lifeline. When God didn't provide "seven action steps to ensure that your adoptive family is exactly as it should be," I was able to see my inadequacy. More than that, I became willing to accept God's call to total surrender.

Total surrender is not a giving up on yourself and your family; it's releasing to your Father the cries held so deep in your heart, you can't breathe. Much like releasing the seeds of a dandelion into the rays of sun on a summer day, surrendering your cries to the son results in something beautiful. As with any other call from the Lord, his intention has always been to receive our openness to his will.

DID I HEAR THAT RIGHT?

*You, LORD, are our Father; your name is Our Redeemer
from Ancient Times.*
—Isaiah 63:16b

IT WAS A FEW MINUTES after yelling at my kids for the first time (yes, the *first* time). They had finally moved into our home, although months before they had moved into our hearts. I was thrilled but anxious. For the agency to recommend us to the judge as adoptive parents, we needed to walk through six months of "supervision." We still had five months to go. So, a wave of panic set in with the realization that their joyful shouts were no longer coming from the back yard!

First racing to each of their bedrooms, then I practically flew down the stairs to the playroom in our basement. No kids! Yanking open the back door, and running toward the opposite side of the barn, there was the sight of bicycles, a jump rope, and a basketball. All items one would expect with children in the vicinity. But, no kids! My shallow breath could barely whisper a prayer.

Then came a sound from a distance. It was a chorus of several children's voices laughing and cheering. Peeking around a vast white pine, I saw them. All three "not quite mine" children had met the neighbor children and joined in for some fun on their trampoline.

My anger grew while marching toward the happy group. And I honestly don't know why. Most parents would have been so relieved that they would have joined in the fun. But that was not the case for me. I stopped at the edge of the trampoline, unable to speak. And, it was clear to each of the children that I was furious.

Although I don't remember exactly what was spoken at that moment, it went something like this: "You need to get your little behinds back over where you belong." And what happened next is something I will never forget.

Three frightened children ran back to our house and disappeared inside. While following them back, I tried to pull myself together to explain why they must always ask before leaving our yard. Once inside the house, the weight of my reaction hit me.

It's hard to know their story and not feel sad.

All three kids were huddled together and trying to remain hidden under a bed. Their eyes were huge, and their faces were frozen in fear. What must they have been thinking?

Admittedly, that was not my finest hour as a new mother. From time to time, I still catch myself with a heavy heart, remembering that day and days after, where I have failed to be the perfect mother. It's hard to know their story and not feel sad. It's also hard to know their story and cut myself a break when I get angry with them.

REFLECTIONS

Countless are the number of times I've checked in with the Lord to make sure I heard him correctly when we chose adoption. His answer has not changed. It's time to change my prayers from self-damning to God-redeeming. Is it time for *you* to change your thinking, as well?

PRAYER:

Abba Father, you have called and equipped me to love and nurture some of your deeply wounded kids. Help my Momma heart to remember that truth when it feels like I misunderstood your voice. Teach me to lean into you through every moment of every day and see my children through your eyes. Amen.

THE CRIES OF YOUR HEART:

_____

_____

_____

_____

_____

_____

_____

_____

USE ONLY AS DIRECTED

*Indeed, this is our boast: The testimony of our
consciences is that we have conducted ourselves in the
world, and especially toward you, with godly sincerity
and purity, not by human wisdom but by God's grace.*
−2 Corinthians 1:12

I USED TO BE one of them. You know who I mean;
they're at the grocery store and in the family
restaurant. They roll their eyes and huff loudly. You
may have heard them whisper, "Someone needs to take
that child in hand."

You pretend you don't hear, as you try to hide your
already-flushed cheeks. These people are strangers.
They don't know that your little boy was born addicted
to drugs. They don't know that his "normal" looking
body has a brain that was interrupted in its
development. They don't know that taking him "in
hand" will escalate his already out-of-control
emotions. They don't know. I didn't.

Perhaps your experience has been like mine. You're
sitting in a restaurant, attempting to have a "family"
dinner after just experiencing a thirty-minute tantrum
back home. And it was a tantrum that included bite
marks on your leg and rug burns on your child from
where she thrashed around in a fit. They will not
understand when asking about what happened to her
arm, and she says it's where her mommy hit her.

Sure, you used to try to explain, with the hope that someone, somewhere, would be on your side. But you've given up the possibility that anyone will ever understand or even care to understand. You've tried their suggestions. You've accepted the books they offered. You've also considered that someone else should be raising your children.

I did. I gave up, even suggesting to my husband that perhaps our children would be better off with their biological family! To which my amazing man responded with a snort and a cough.

Satan throws out lies for us to stumble on.

It seems that at any time, while a person moves forward along a path they believe is directed by God, Satan throws out lies for us to stumble on. He is a master at planting doubt. And then, we allow others to water and fertilize those seeds of doubt until they grow into the certainty that we are wrong.

REFLECTIONS

Will you join me in deciding to listen *only* to God's opinion? Let's press on with what we know is right for *our* families.

PRAYER:

Lord, God, it often feels like everyone else knows better than I do how to parent my struggling children. Help me to remember the words of a fellow adoptive mom that my sole responsibility is to do as you have directed. Since my children are on loan from you, my parenting only needs your approval. Seal your truth on my heart and mind, so that I may remember you are in the middle of even the most painful situations. Amen.

THE CRIES OF YOUR HEART:

_____

_____

_____

_____

_____

_____

_____

_____

FATHER KNOWS BEST

Don't be like them, because your Father knows the things you need before you ask him.
−Matthew 6:8

THE MOMENT my bottom connected with the seat, he crawled into my lap. Burying his face into my shoulder, his nine-year-old body shook with swallowed sobs. It had been a tough day. His recent attempts at mouthing off had fallen flat. I guided him into the nearest room with a door for some privacy. His angry rants turned to burning, tearful apologies. Except he wasn't sorry for this recent misbehavior; he was sorry that he had told. My sweet boy mistakenly believed that his family of origin was torn apart because of him.

It made no difference to remind him of all the things he had done right.

In that particular moment, I held him tightly and rocked him gently, praying that Jesus would help my son see the truth. And I invited him, not for the first time, to tell me the story. It made no difference to remind him of all the things he had done right. He still believed the lie.

So many children, in so much pain, believe lies about their story. When there is not a mature adult available to provide supporting answers, wounded children create their own truth. A self-damning lie becomes a reality, no matter what we say.

REFLECTIONS

Instead of burdening ourselves with an impossible task of erasing false beliefs, let's lift our children to the Lord, who already knows what they need.

PRAYER:

Lord, so often, I must acknowledge that there is nothing I can do to mend broken hearts. But You know precisely what my children and I need at this moment...and in the next...and in the next...and in the next. You know what it feels like to be defeated and broken. Help me to know your sweet presence even now. Jesus, big brother, your little sister needs you. Let me feel your embrace, your love, your peace, so that I may rest in you as I point my children to your truth. Amen.

THE CRIES OF YOUR HEART:

_____

_____

_____

_____

_____

_____

_____

_____

_____

WE'RE NOT SO DIFFERENT

We wait for the Lord; he is our help and shield.
—Psalm 33:20

THERE'S A STACK of lined journals, filled with my various adventures, thoughts, and prayers spanning from my Freshman year of college through today. There are occasions when something catches my eye while flipping through one of them. Recently, a particular paragraph jumped off a page at me. It read:

"I keep my kids, husband, and friends a safe distance from my heart. I'm tired of being hurt and disappointed. It feels like I don't have the discernment to know when someone is mistreating me. I try to be always preparing for someone, anyone to reject me. I believe that somehow it will hurt less that way. I must be missing out on so much."

As I read through to the end of the entry, it occurred to me how easily this could be the written thoughts of any one of my children. Except they do not realize they believe such lies. Children who come through trauma have survived so much pain and rejection, abuse, and neglect, separation from primary bonds. They have never had someone available to help sort through their junk. They don't even know what parts are junk and what parts are not.

So, when we take them into our homes, into our arms, into our hearts, they resist. Who's to say we would be any different? Ultimately, we do life as adoptive mommas on a tight rope. A heavy sigh stirs anxiety for one. The slightest possibility of a "no" can trigger an all-out meltdown tantrum for a twelve-year-old. Looking at this book instead of at that particularly insecure child might lead to rage.

Everything feels like rejection– even love. Just like me, and probably just like you, they are trying to avoid being hurt. Not the physical kind of hurt, the internal type that makes your heart pound and your belly sick. Knowing that I have experienced only a sliver of what my kids have endured and that I wanted to die from the hurt, gives me a clearer perspective on what thoughts are behind their actions. I can't *fix* it, and I don't like that.

I can't fix it, and I don't like that.

How many times have you experienced a lashing out from one of your kiddos and thought, "He's just being a jerk"? How often do you cry out to God and ask, "Why won't she just let me love her"? When was the last time you lamented to your spouse, "I'm screwing up this Mom gig"?

These thoughts come almost every day. Frequently I'll make promises to myself about doing better to protect my heart. But I'm tired. Are you?

REFLECTIONS

Will you join me in the practice of waiting on the Lord to be our help and shield so we can love our kids without fear?

PRAYER:

God and Father surround my family with your shield. Remind the enemy, Satan, and his minions that he is already defeated by the life, death, and resurrection of Jesus Christ. Enable me to know your peace like never before and to lay down a clear path for my family. Thank you for understanding my needs before I even ask and for answering in the perfect way. Amen.

THE CRIES OF YOUR HEART:

_____

_____

_____

_____

_____

_____

_____

_____

LIGHTS WORK BETTER WHEN THE LAMP IS PLUGGED IN

The Lord is my light and my salvation—whom should I fear? The Lord is the stronghold of my life—whom should I dread?
—Psalm 27:1

IT'S NO SECRET around the Nagel house that I try to accomplish too many things at once. I am often thinking of project number three or four while executing task number one. As a result, my family has found some rather curious things around the house.

Once I transferred the laundry from the washer to the dryer, but found it still wet the next morning because the dryer was never actually started! We have eaten dinner an hour or two later than expected because although I preheated the oven and set the timer, I never actually moved the casserole off the counter and into the oven. Everyone is quick to extend grace toward me in those moments. But, I'm not so great at going easy on myself because of the genuinely unrealistic expectations I have regarding my performance as a wife and mother.

> *I had laid the groundwork for those impractical expectations for a very long time.*

If you were to look back over my life, you would discover that I had laid the groundwork for those impractical expectations for a very long time. To me, it was somehow virtuous to always strive for perfection. Then our kids came along. It didn't take me long to realize that they pay much more attention to what I am doing than to what I am saying.

When my daughter wanted to help prepare dinner one evening, I gave her a step stool, an apron, and a simple task. That first stroke down of the peeler resulted in the carrot flying in one direction and the peeler in another. I chuckled and was about to say something silly when I looked at the face of my sweet girl and saw tears. She was trembling and struggling to take a deep breath. It was clear that she had observed my own self-criticism and assumed my feelings toward her would be the same. What's more, kids who have lived with more than one family are often wondering, even worrying, that the arrangement won't stick, and someone might give them back.

At that moment, the Lord quickly gave me the right words, and I said, "Yay! Welcome to Mom's Kitchen, where it's impossible to make food without making a mess." It has taken some time, but that sweet little miss has found confidence in knowing that mistakes happen, that life is messy, and that we are still family.

It's almost uncanny how we can forget, as believers, that life in Christ is more than just salvation from the torment of Hell. Christ is our source of life and light. You can place a lamp on a table in a dark room, install a new bulb, and turn on the switch. But if you don't plug the lamp into its power source, the light will not fill the room.

REFLECTIONS

You can know the lamp is there, yet still not benefit from its radiance. You can know the electrical source is there but believe the enemy when he tells you the lamp doesn't work. The devil will gladly provide you with all sorts of lies to convince you that darkness is inevitable. He wants to keep our families from living in the light. Let's plug into our real source of light, Jesus Christ.

PRAYER:

Lord, you are Light, and you are Life. You are Truth. You are more powerful than anything Satan tries to inflict on my family. Make your will and presence known in clear and compelling ways. Let only your will be done and let your peace and truth settle all around me. Amen.

THE CRIES OF YOUR HEART:

_____

_____

_____

_____

_____

_____

_____

_____

SOMETHING'S NOT RIGHT HERE

*Wisdom and strength belong to God; counsel and
understanding are his.*
–Job 12:13

IMAGINE THIS: A little girl, who is not yet a year old, is removed from her primary home and placed in the arms of strangers who proceed to ignore her for the next two years. When she comes to you, she has just turned three. She has not been trained to use the toilet. She has not yet spoken more than a few simple words.

When you take her into your home and into your heart, you look into her big blue eyes, knowing that you will do everything necessary to meet her needs. This includes combing the internet for answers, asking questions in forums, and interviewing other adoptive parents. You read stacks of books from the library and express your concerns to family, friends, or anyone who will listen. And their responses always come back with the same theme: Give her time. Give her time. Give her time.

After a while, you begin to lose hope that you'll find answers. You feel inadequate. You may even question whether you should be her mother. But, some part of you says, "NO! Something's just not right."

She talks now, although haltingly. She mostly makes it to the bathroom on time. Still, you know something is wrong. You wonder why no one else can see it. Then you remember the one thing you forgot: to ask the Lord for guidance. Soon after, you hear about a place that provides testing for children like yours, and you prayerfully make the call.

...you remember the one thing you forgot: to ask the Lord for guidance.

Sitting behind a glass window at a big university, a specialized team interviews your little girl, who is now six. Did you waste too much time? You seek the Lord's wisdom. A few hours later, the truth is revealed. Solutions are in place, and you can breathe again—at least for today.

REFLECTIONS

So often, I find myself turning to prayer as a last resort when it comes to my kids. It's as if seeking God means I have failed and must crawl to Him in shame. It occurs to me that perhaps God placed my children with precisely the right momma because He knew I would grow tired of parenting failures born of my own strength and eventually run to Him for answers. Maybe, just maybe, He's okay with imperfect parents like me.

PRAYER:

God, you are all-wise and all-powerful. Nothing is impossible for you. You know every situation, and you know exactly what needs to happen. I choose to pray with confidence that you will meet me in even the tiniest place of uncertainty. Give me answers. Give me peace. Give me rest. Bring your healing. Amen.

THE CRIES OF YOUR HEART:

_____

_____

_____

_____

_____

_____

_____

_____

I CAN'T DO THIS ANYMORE

We love because he first loved us.
−1 John 4:19

WHEN OUR TRIO FIRST CAME to live in our home, my husband and I knew that we needed to quickly lay out some ground rules and establish clear expectations. We sat together around the dining room table and gave each child a chance to provide input. The moment was sometimes silly and sometimes serious, but we eventually came up with a list to which everyone could agree.

I love each of you. I always will love you.

Then I asked to clarify just one expectation: Love. On my part, I had fallen in love with them the moment I viewed that email attachment containing their picture. It occurred to me, however, that they should not be made to feel like their love toward my husband and myself is a requirement for them.

"I love each of you. I always will love you. Sometimes getting into trouble from Dad or me will not feel like love because love is not just a feeling; it's also a choice. I already love you, and I always will, but you are not required to love me. I hope that one day you will choose to love me, but it is entirely your choice."

Not much was said after that, and we moved on with our day.

Looking back over the years, although it was the right thing to say, boy do I wish I hadn't! I say that tongue in cheek because each of the three have tested me on it over and over. I have been kicked and left with mouth-shaped bruises resulting from bites to my arm or leg. I've overheard big brother tell his little sisters, "They aren't our real parents. They are not our family."

Once, after jumping to a wrong conclusion, I penned a note of apology to one of my kiddos. But they were already asleep in bed. The next morning, I found my note torn to pieces on my kitchen counter. I have cried myself to sleep on countless nights, not only feeling unloved by each child but also despised and rejected. Then I remember Jesus. He loved us first even though he knew he would be despised, rejected, and ultimately murdered.

Jesus loved us first, even though he knew there would be times when we would make the wrong choice, only because we could. Each of us has beaten up on Jesus and his love in our own ways. Why is that? I think it's because we struggle to believe he is any different than any other person who has disappointed or harmed us.

We want to believe his love for us is true and real but have a very skewed understanding of love. Our kids who started life in trauma are no different. Love is a big scary word that can quickly bring pain and rejection. They will use it sparingly. You and I must choose to model Christ and allow him to reveal his love for our adopted children.

REFLECTIONS

Together, let's agree to walk in the perfection of the Lord's love for us, so that our children may observe and experience His love for themselves.

PRAYER:

Great God, the Scripture says that we love because you loved us first. I have come to realize that therapeutic parenting is too hard for me to do on my own. Help me remember that you never expected me to love in my own strength as if love were a school assignment. The love of Christ compels me to love. Teach me in a new way how to experience Christ's love, so that I cannot help but love these children who, in their own pain, often reject me. Amen.

THE CRIES OF YOUR HEART:

PACKAGES WRAPPED WITH RIBBONS AND BOWS

He predestined us to be adopted as sons through Jesus Christ for himself, according to the good pleasure of his will, to the praise of his glorious grace that he lavished on us in the Beloved One.
—Ephesians 1: 5-6

I WALKED AROUND department store after store in search of the perfect birthday gift for an 11-year-old girl who had walked through and continues to work through the damaging horrors of trauma. My greatest desire was to give her something that would repair and restore her childhood. She enjoys so many things, but mainly those related to horses.   She LOVES horses—books about horses, dolls who ride horses, and collectible toy horses.

So, the task should have been easy, right? Not so much. Everything I spotted for her left me feeling empty. These were just things. One lesson I learned early in my childhood was, "Never hold tightly to things."   And research *...they quickly learn that nothing is forever.* shows that when a child is placed in an uncertain environment, after forcibly being removed from their birth home (*with only the clothes on their back*), they quickly learn that nothing is forever. Everything they have ever been given is now fair game for every other child around. What could be bought to fix that?

Although I didn't want to buy them, I eventually chose Barbie dolls. Shopping had made me weary and empty. Why was this so difficult for me? Did I really believe that a birthday gift would make or break my sometimes-volatile relationship with my daughter? Yes. I really did believe that.

Years before, my pastor had preached, "The best gift to give your family is a walk with God, worth imitating." Thinking back to his advice caused me to pause with a gulp! It was difficult to swallow with the big lump in my throat. At that moment, I realized my gifts to the family didn't line up with what my pastor's wise advice.

Instead, I was gifting them anxiety over my apparent failure as a mom. The packages were wrapped with good intentions that were actually broken and sour. The only gift to repair and restore the traumatic past for each of my children is a relationship with the Lord. I'm planning on making that a gift every day.

REFLECTIONS

Does shopping for your children make you weary? What gifts do you give them? Are they gifts that will last for eternity?

PRAYER:

God of grace, thank you for how lavish and generous you are with your love toward me. Teach me to receive it. Teach me to express it and lead my steps in teaching the young souls in my home that your love comes with no strings attached. Amen.

THE CRIES OF YOUR HEART:

_____

_____

_____

_____

_____

_____

_____

_____

YOU'RE LOOKING THE WRONG WAY

Love is patient, love is kind. Love does not envy, is not boastful, is not arrogant, is not rude, is not self-seeking, is not irritable, and does not keep a record of wrongs.
−1 Corinthians 13: 4-5

WHEN MY SON WAS AROUND TEN YEARS OLD, he decided to test out "back talk." It didn't go well the first few times, because I was able to ignore it. So, he tried harder and harder and harder. Although the training provided by our adoption agency taught that it was best not to react, a woman can only take so much.

After a string of his particularly vile and cutting comments, I snapped—well, more likely yelled, "I realize that we have given you permission to choose whether or not you will love us. But you WILL respect me!"

Yes, yelling at someone to gain their respect never works, but I didn't think that through. My son stormed off to his room, sobbing as though he'd just been beaten to within an inch of his life. I stormed off to my room, crying for being such a big jerk and for taking the bait.

After calming down, willing to own my mistakes, I wrote my son a note. We often write notes to each other in our family as a way to connect without any real expectations. My words read, "I love you even when you are in trouble," and the note was written in red – his favorite color. I gently slipped it under his bedroom door and headed off to do some gardening (*because those darn weeds sure aren't going to pull themselves*)!

...let's keep Him in our line of sight and lean into Him for truth and direction.

When it was time to start prepping for dinner, I returned to the house, got myself cleaned up, and headed for the kitchen. While tying my apron, I noticed an envelope on the counter. Inside was the note I had written to my son, now torn into tiny jagged pieces. His message was clear. My heart sank, as it had so many times before, and I cried.

I'm convinced that a large part of why we get so hurt and frustrated by the poor choices and behaviors of our trauma kids is because we allow them to become *our* failure and, ultimately, *our* identity. I had failed to love my hurting child correctly; therefore, I was a failure and a bad parent. This results in us entering their world of pain and fear, instead of us inviting them to join our world of grace and peace.

REFLECTIONS

If we take our eyes off God, who is Love, we teach our children to do the same when times get tough. Instead, let's keep Him in our line of sight and lean into Him for truth and direction.

PRAYER:

Dear God, author of love, you keep no record of my wrongs. Show me how to train my mind to rely on your love—particularly in those moments when I feel so unloved by children who are afraid to love. Use me, as you see fit, to direct my challenging kids into your waiting arms. Teach me to keep my eyes always on you and your perfect love. Amen.

THE CRIES OF YOUR HEART:

_____

_____

_____

_____

_____

_____

_____

_____

THERE'S ALWAYS HOPE

For you are my hope, Lord God, my confidence from my youth.
–Psalm 71:5

OUR FIRST CHRISTMAS as a family was amazing. The judge had ordered our adoption finalized just seven days earlier. There were so many gifts around our tree. Packages had arrived from our family in other states. The agency we worked with had arranged for another family to "sponsor" our first Christmas by providing toys and clothes. And of course, my husband and I had purchased items as well.

Dad read the story of the first Christmas from the Gospel of Luke. Mom led the singing of Happy Birthday, Jesus. The turkey was in the oven, and snow was lightly falling. Cheers and shouts of joy and laughter filled our once empty home. I remember thinking that I never expected the opportunity to be a mother to feel so–so–I have no words for how good it felt. I'll cherish those early moments forever.

I have no words for how good it felt.

The trouble with trying to build a family with kids who began their life traumatically is that they are not able to trust what feels like love. They can only take so much of the good feelings before their survival instinct kicks in, and they are suddenly on high alert. And on this wonderful Christmas morning, I didn't know this yet. So, when my ideal Christmas started crashing down all around—when the joy and laughter turned to tantrums and tears—my heart sank into my stomach. It was the first of many nights I would go to bed crying.

We have learned quite a bit since that first Christmas together. The main lesson being that we must do what works for our family. Christmas, we eventually realized, is not the only holiday that looks different from most. After two or three years of horrific experiences on Mother's Day, I finally canceled it. We don't celebrate Mother's Day in the same way as other families. We stay home from church (gasp!). We don't go out for brunch. There are no handmade cards, no flowers.

Instead, we celebrate Mother's Day by ignoring it. I take a nap and spend the day in pajamas and slippers. I still have a deep sadness in my heart for what might have been. But I refuse to live my life in the shadow of a woman I have never met. I will not ask my children to celebrate me and forget about the woman who gave them life. There is grief in their hearts for losing her. Allowing themselves to love me feels too much like they are cheating on her. I won't ask them to do that. Instead, I try to remember to turn to the Lord, who is, after all, my one and only true love.

REFLECTIONS

What about you? Are you torturing yourself by trying to be all that your kids need and more? Are you placing your hope for the future happiness of your family on your ability to "win" them? Please stop. I urge you to stop. God has always been and always will be the only one who is enough. Rest in Him and his love for you. Then, any love that comes from your kids is bonus love.

PRAYER:

God of hope, sometimes parenting kids coming from difficult places of trauma, feels so hopeless. The greater the effort I put into loving and bonding, the stronger their fear and rejection. Help me abide in you and your love. Yours is not a place without hope. Help me to lay my children and their pain into your loving arms. Fill me with the confidence that you are everything our family needs. YOU are hope. Amen

THE CRIES OF YOUR HEART:

_____

_____

_____

_____

_____

_____

_____

_____

_____

OUT OF CONTROL

Compassion and forgiveness belong to the Lord our God, though we have rebelled against him.
−Daniel 9:9

THE THIRD TIME my daughter ran away from home, she was only eight. It came after correcting her about table manners, something minor in a traditional family setting. In our house, every correction can mean danger and rejection. It doesn't matter how much we affirm that there is nothing they can do to make us send them away, our kids still panic after almost six years! A raised voice, an irritated sigh, a sharp correction is as frightening to them as if we were charging at them with a weapon.

I know this. I observe this. Yet even still, I lose my cool. Knowing myself full well, on this particular day, my correction probably went something like, "Why do we have to do battle over the tiniest of things around here?" And after those words left my mouth, I walked away.

But somehow, my daughter heard my words more like, "If you can't even get your table manners right, then I don't want you anymore. You are ruining our otherwise perfect family."

No exaggeration. I know this because of the note she left. "I'm sorry I keep messing up our family. I think you will all be better off without me." My animal-loving little girl had decided she would go live with the calves at the dairy farm nearby.

Thankfully, we can chuckle a little about it now, but on that day, she was dead serious. We found her halfway between our house and the pasture. She had tried to wade through some brambles, but they grabbed her skin and hair and held her tight.

Approaching the spot where she was struggling, bleeding, and sobbing, I was so angry. It would have felt good to yell at her and remind her of all the ways she had put herself in danger. Perhaps I could scare her into never running away again.

What can I do to make you see just how much I love you?

But instead, once I saw her predicament, I pulled her to me and cried. And she cried. I told her, "What can I do to make you see just how much I love you?" She didn't answer, probably because she didn't know the answer.

We have grown much in our relationship since that day. Yes, we have continued to struggle. There have been times when she has been annoyed with me or when I have been irritated with her. But parents must be ready to apologize when they're in the wrong. And she has been quick to ask me over and over to affirm my love for her.

Truthfully, I can't do it—at least not on my own. Not without allowing Christ who lives in me to live through me. It all works much better when it is done like that.

How many hard moments have escalated into horrible moments because you lost your cool? How many times have you dug your feet in and refused to budge, determined to win at least one battle?

REFLECTIONS

Our anger comes from fear. In our fear of failing as parents, we choose anger because it feels so much more powerful than fear. What are you afraid of? What makes you angry? What if you didn't have to fight anymore because you let Jesus have the fear and the control?

PRAYER:

Forgiving God, I admit that I can become so irritable with my children, especially as they struggle through the muck of their early lives. Your word is clear that irritability is not love. Forgive me. Rather than be "irritable," teach me to be "imperturbable." Remind me that in the depths of their behavior lies a pain so sharp only you can understand and heal. Give me what I need to carry them to you, no matter how difficult. Amen.

THE CRIES OF YOUR HEART:

_____

_____

_____

_____

_____

_____

_____

_____

SOMEBODY'S WATCHING OVER ME

So, she named the Lord who spoke to her: "You are El-Roi," for she said, "In this place, have I actually seen the one who sees me?"
—Genesis 16:13

ON OUR WEDDING DAY, before the ceremony, the minister met with my soon-to-be-husband and me individually for prayer. He gave a piece of advice that, at the time, seemed sweet and poetic. He told us to take mental "snapshots" of the beautiful moments that come with marriage. Then we could pull out our proverbial albums and remember the good times when life got ugly.

With God's help, that advice has gotten us through some tumultuous times in our marriage. Similarly, when I get bogged down with the weight of therapeutic parenting, it is good to look back in my journal to our early days as a family—to the days when it was all fresh and exciting. It is in those snapshots where the memory of specific moments keeps me going:

> April 18th, 2014, Good Friday: We walked into a meeting with our social worker. I was only expecting to meet more people who are involved in the kids' lives (which did happen). Then our

worker gave us the news that the State of Michigan gave her the approval she needed to make us parents! I'm still shocked. We are going to meet our kids for the first time on May 1st! I can't believe it.

May 1st, 2014: We met our kids for the first time today. I love them already and can hardly wait to bring them home for good. There is a part of me that is so scared. I'm afraid I'll really blow it. Part of me is excited. I want to love on them and show them the love of Jesus. Some of my friends assure me the mixed feelings are evidence of a mother's heart. We hope to have them with us full time by Father's Day.

I remember all the excitement and all the anticipation. God was answering my prayer of becoming a mother. I pictured myself hugging them, tickling them, and peacefully tucking them in at night after bedtime prayers. And thankfully, those thoughts have become a reality many times since then. What a treasure to capture those beautiful snapshots, mainly because they are not easily earned. Love and trust are precious commodities for my little ones.

Love and trust are precious commodities for my little ones.

REFLECTIONS

What are your "snapshots?" Do you need to spend time looking through albums while asking God to be the bond in your family relationships?

PRAYER:

El Roi, you are the God who sees me. You see just how desperately I long to share an exchange of love with my children. It's not as easy as I think it should be. I can't do it on my own. I need you to show me their hearts from your perspective and show me the steps to take to meet them there. Teach me to stop trying so hard in my human strength and to begin resting in your desire to love them through me. Amen.

THE CRIES OF YOUR HEART:

_____

_____

_____

_____

_____

_____

_____

_____

SUCKER PUNCH

Therefore, as God's chosen ones, holy and dearly loved,
put on compassion, kindness, humility, gentleness, and
patience, bearing with one another and forgiving one
another if anyone has a grievance against another.
Just as the Lord has forgiven you,
so you are also to forgive.
−Colossians 3:12-13

THE MOMENT I HEARD the words that came out of my daughter's mouth, I knew they didn't originate from her. The vocabulary was a little too grown-up, and the concepts quite off from her regular radar. Like every other conversation with my kids, I had to breathe deep and check my tone if I was going to get to the bottom of the issue.

As casually as possible, I asked, "Where did you hear that from?" Her answer shocked me like a stiff punch to the gut. She named my friend. At the beginning of my life as an adoptive mother, I assumed that the people who knew me the best and cared about me the most would understand why we do things differently. And that they would respect that.

But instead, what unfolded that afternoon was a string of stories about conversations between my friend and my children when I was not present. Aside from my husband and sister, this was the one person I trusted to be alone with my children. Yet she had been undermining my work in bonding our family, with her opinions of what I was doing wrong. She had betrayed me!

Worse yet, she had betrayed my children by placing them in a position they should never have to endure. My kids already struggle over divided loyalties between their birth mother and me. This made me angry. I was hurt and felt nauseated.

Later, when I told my husband about the situation, as usual, he wanted me to confront her. But I didn't. Confrontation has always been a difficult thing for me. And in this instance, a confrontation wasn't the answer because a part of me believed my friend was correct.

Maybe I am too strict. Perhaps the kids shouldn't have chores. Should they have more freedom to watch television and play video games? Was I too protective in not allowing overnighters? Or was I simply a failure at mothering children that were hurting? Clearly, this person knew better than me!

...a confrontation wasn't the answer...

So, I did what I do best in my fleshly ways—withdrew. I stopped returning calls and no longer dropped by. I gave it all up. But it didn't help the situation.

As it turned out, I spoke with some fellow adoptive moms who had walked through the same kind of hurt. Each of them had handled it in their own way. But the part that struck me the most, as we sipped coffee and shared our burdens, was their tongue-in-cheek comment, "Congratulations! Now you are a real adoptive mother. Welcome to the club!"

REFLECTIONS

Navigating through the murky waters as adoptive parents can be unbearably painful. It's natural for any human to reach out for help, encouragement, or prayer. But when that results in a stinging response, we stop reaching. If we keep our eyes on the people around us and their opinions, we will continually struggle. Doing life in the flesh never lasts. If we turn to Christ as our source for truth and strength, our relationships with those who think they understand can become opportunities to bring about an understanding of the world of trauma.

PRAYER:

Merciful Father, your love is kind. I fail again and again to respond with loving kindness in a tense moment. Honestly, it feels more natural to be defensive. Teach me today to walk in your truth and compassion, trusting your Spirit in me to demonstrate your loving ways. Amen.

THE CRIES OF YOUR HEART:

ATTITUDE ADJUSTMENT

*Patience is better than power and controlling one's
emotions than capturing a city.*
—Proverbs 16:32

I SNAPPED AT MY SON for the umpteenth time
that day. It was a Saturday, and he asked if we had any
plans for the day. My swift and cutting response was,
"It is not my job to entertain you. Sometimes nothing
is going on, and we just need to stay home. I promise
it won't kill you to play outside today."

He wisely did not respond to my short rant. For
another two minutes or so, I felt fully justified in being
harsh with him. After all, everything
I said was right. I was tired and
hadn't slept well the night before.
He dared to ask such a question
before I even made the coffee!

*He was not
to blame for
my tired
mind and
body.*

Enter the Holy Spirit—that gentle,
still, and small voice that never
shames me but always challenges
me. There was no doubt about it, I had wronged my
son. He was not to blame for my tired mind and body.
He's just the child in our family who likes to know
ahead of time how the day will unfold.

After getting dressed for the day, and before making
coffee, I walked outside to where he was practicing

free throws. I waited for him to notice me, but he said nothing when he did.

"I owe you an apology," I said. "I had no right to snap at you earlier when you were just asking a simple question. Although I'm extra tired, that is no excuse. I'm sorry; please know that I'm always working on me."

He still didn't say a word but went back to his basketball, and I went back inside. It's unclear how much time passed, but eventually, my sweet boy came inside and said, "Hi Mommy," and hugged me in the tightest bear hug he could manage. True forgiveness.

I remember learning from a pastor and mentor that transparency can minister to the hearts of those around you if you are willing. Though I am not encouraging anyone to lay out their entire thought life before their adopted children, you are encouraged to be real. Be humble. Be honest.

REFLECTIONS

The words "I'm sorry. I messed up. I hope you can forgive me," say so much to our children. At the very least, those words help us acknowledge our own shortcomings. Stating them allows our children to see that our relationship with them is essential to us. Don't try to be perfect; be humble.

PRAYER:

Abba, love is patient. So many times, I need to be patient in love for my children. I feel weary, even on the best days. Help me to rest in you and to live out an attitude of patience that will give my kids the space they need to grow in you, at the perfect pace you have laid out for them. Amen.

THE CRIES OF YOUR HEART:

_____

_____

_____

_____

_____

_____

_____

_____

_____

IT'S TIME FOR A DEMONSTRATION

Though the mountains move and the hills shake, my love will not be removed from you, and my covenant of peace will not be shaken," says your compassionate Lord.
—Isaiah 54:10

THE WINTER WIND bit at his face, and a shiver ran up his spine. Hoping and praying that today would be different, he rounded the corner to the bus stop and immediately dropped his little sister's gloved hand.

Shoot! The other kids were already there, laughing as they tried to push each other off the curb. Maybe looking straight ahead would prevent any teasing. It didn't. Almost as quickly as the thought came, so did the snow to the back of his head.

Two older girls, who were exceptionally cruel, packed chunks of ice into their snowballs. The boy didn't engage except to try and block his sister from the painful projectiles. "Hey, Foster Kid! Foster Kid! I'm talking to you. Do you even know your real name?" Laughing voices all around offered up a combination of spiteful suggestions.

At last, the bus arrived. Children scrambled for their book bags and jostled for the first position in line. Relieved that he had managed to withhold his tears, my son stepped back and ushered his sister onboard before climbing the steps. On Saturday, the doorbell chimed, announcing neighborhood kids in search of more playmates.

My son said, "I still have to do my chores." then closed the door and walked away. Something was off. This boy, this child who had only been my son for six months, never turned down an opportunity to play outside.

Raising an eyebrow, I asked, "What's up with that?"

His tears came quickly and turned into sobs. Pulling him toward me for a safe hug, I waited. He resisted at first and then leaned in. Between the sobs and gasps for air, he choked out his story.

My son told me about the teasing and the ice balls. He shared how each school day, he would stand at the bus stop trying to ignore them because "Dad said to never hit girls."

Wrapping ourselves in warm blankets, we snuggled into the couch and talked about when it is better to "let it go," and when it is important to tell an adult. This was something he had never known until then. Kids from traumatic backgrounds typically don't know how to advocate for themselves, or even if they are allowed to do so.

If you don't teach them, they probably won't know.

If you don't teach them, they probably won't know. Until the day my sweet boy broke down, I assumed this phrase referred to self-care and basic life skills, such as brushing your teeth or frying an egg. Our deeply wounded kids need guidance in EVERY aspect of life to transition from surviving to thriving.

REFLECTIONS

Do you catch yourself making assumptions regarding what your kids know? Do you say things like, "He should know that by now?" Can you lay down your expectations of how it should be and join me in seeking God's direction?

PRAYER:

God and Father of compassion, you have loved me with an unshakable love. You have instructed us to love one another in the same way that Christ loves us. Teach me to love my children the way you have loved me. Some days it is so difficult to love someone as they push that love away. As they reject me for daring to connect with them, teach me to see things from your perspective. Empower me to love my children in a way that demonstrates your love. Amen.

THE CRIES OF YOUR HEART:

_____

_____

_____

_____

_____

_____

_____

_____

DISASTER AVERTED

"For I know the plans I have for you"—this is the Lord's declaration—"plans for your well-being, not for disaster, to give you a future and a hope."
—Jeremiah 29:11

IT IS SO ENJOYABLE listening to my girls as they get ready for church on Sunday morning. Their bathroom is right beside my bedroom, and I can generally hear them talking about what to wear. Should they match today? Should they wear their hair up or down? It makes my heart smile to watch them grow up as friends. Sister friends are the best.

Perhaps I could learn a few things from these girls, who've been through so much, and at such a young age. They do so well at living in the current moment, while I'm busy borrowing trouble from the future. It's always been that way for me, probably to feel less fear of the unknown. And my borrowing trouble has become even more pronounced since adopting children.

Not only do I worry about whether they will succeed in school, I worry about how my eight-year-old will manage a career with such severe dyslexia. When my son makes a wrong choice or just acts like a fool, I fear that he will follow those who have gone before him down a path toward prison.

It's always been that way for me...

When chores don't get done, I'm convinced that my children will never hold a job because they won't do what they are told!

Having heard so many stories from fellow adoptive moms about Children's Services suddenly showing up at the front door, I find myself wondering if I'm next. As a result, my relationships suffer through worrying about things I can't control. It puts a distance between my children and me for fear I'll say or do the wrong thing. Confiding in my husband is rare because when I'm overwhelmed with parenting, there's the fear that he will get fed up and stop coming home. There's even a hesitancy to make new friendships because I'm convinced that, "Everyone grows tired of me eventually." A pretty fun way to live, eh?

REFLECTIONS

One of the amazing things about the Word of God is its relevance across generations and situations. I can look at the ancient words of promise and know that the Lord already knows my future. I don't need to borrow trouble as some clumsy attempt to feel in control. I can live in hope. What about you? Do you borrow trouble? Are you ready to stop?

PRAYER:

Eternal God, you hold my future. You hold the future of my children. Your plan is for us to have HOPE for the future. Use me to teach my children to dream big, run strong, soar on wings like eagles, and believe that God is always bigger, stronger, and more powerful than anything that weighs them down. Amen.

THE CRIES OF YOUR HEART:

_____

_____

_____

_____

_____

_____

_____

_____

LAUGHTER IS
THE BEST MEDICINE

*Our mouths were filled with laughter then, and our
tongues with shouts of joy. Then they said among the
nations, "The Lord has done great things for them."*
−Psalm 126:2

WE WERE LAUGHING SO HARD, I wet my pants.
What is it with dogs and their propensity to roll
around on horribly smelling things? The air was
muggy that day. Mosquitoes (*jokingly dubbed the
state bird of Michigan*) were swarming, and we were
all grumpy.

The chicken coop needed cleaning, and not one
of us wanted to do it. Compromising, we agreed to
work together for a quicker finish. Having already
hollered at the dog several times for eating the
chicken droppings (gag) and at the kids for
standing by to watch me work, I was ready to do
battle with the next person who dared to cross me.
Flexing my back, taking a deep breath, and stepping
out of the coop just in time to catch the dog rolling
around on the remnants of a rabbit carcass, I
cursed.

Attempting to stop the dog, one of my girls was
ordered to go fetch the dog shampoo, and the other
sent to turn on the garden spigot. I grabbed Kyla by
the collar, and of course, as soon as the water

started flowing, the dog started squirming. Someone clipped a leash to her collar, trying to prevent escape, while I grumbled something about not letting a nasty smelling dog into my house.

Having had enough, she began shaking herself from the end of her nose to the tip of her tail. Soapy water flew in every direction, showering us all. She ran around behind me to escape the water, which resulted in the leash winding around my legs and taking me down to the muddy, smelly ground.

Not yet satisfied, she gave herself another good shake. We were soaked. Someone started giggling, which turned into laughing, which grew into a howling roar, and my bladder let loose. More laughter, more mess as the dog now ran around the yard, dragging the leash behind her. While I confessed, "I just peed my pants!" Once we were finished laughing, our sides ached. It was a good kind of ache.

Our kids often don't know how to respond in a given situation...

That day of frustration turned to laughter is one of my favorite memories. So much of our time and energy is burned up by the fires of traumatic memories. Our kids often don't know how to respond in a given situation, so they look to us for direction. Later, if we think we didn't demonstrate the "correct" way, we decide that we failed.

REFLECTIONS

Yes, trauma is hard, therapeutic parenting is exhausting, and we persistently feel incapable. Will you permit yourself to laugh? Join me in praying for a sense of humor?

PRAYER:

Creator of joy, laughter, and humor, life is heavy with pain, grief, failure, and loss. Help me teach my children to take their eyes off from the weight of it all and smile at the future and what it holds for them in You. Show me how to experience real joy. Teach me to laugh at myself and find humor in my clumsy ways. Give me the grace I need to show myself the grace my children need to see. Shine your smiling face upon our family and lighten our hearts. Amen.

THE CRIES OF YOUR HEART:

_____

_____

_____

_____

_____

_____

_____

_____

SOMEONE CALL SECURITY!

❧❧❧❧❧❧❧❧❧❧❧❧❧❧❧❧❧

*"He will be like a tree planted by water: it sends its
roots out toward a stream, it doesn't fear when heat
comes, and its foliage remains green. It will not worry
in a year of drought or cease producing fruit."*
—Jeremiah 17:8

"HELP! Somebody help me." His cries seeped through
the bedroom walls like a leak in an overburdened
dam. Frantic to get to my terrified boy, I wrestled out
of the bedsheets. The path around the end of my bed,
across the room, down the hall and to his door
seemed inordinately long.

Sitting up in bed, wide eyes brimming with tears,
my son of only two weeks was terrified. "Hey, Buddy,
I'm here. What's going on? Did you have a bad
dream?" More tears escaped as he nodded. "Do you
want to tell me what's wrong?"

When he still didn't answer, I pulled him close until
the sobbing subsided. Offering him a sip of water, I
kissed his forehead and tucked him in. But as I stood
to leave, the tears flowed anew.

Once again, upright and with fear in his voice, he
held open his empty arms and asked, "Mom, can I put
this down?" His eyes were wide but blank. "It's a gun,
and it's really heavy."

Then it dawned on me, night terrors. His traumatized brain was stuck somewhere between waking and a horribly real dream.

"Of course, you can put it down. Let's put it right over there in the trash, and you never have to pick it up again, ever." Going through the motion of placing the firearm in the bucket, he laid back down, eyes finally closed, and mind restfully asleep.

I am no more living from a place of peace than my children.

There is a level of sadness that comes with parenting kids from painful pasts. The sadness comes in the moments of our remembering their behavior is not a tool for pushing buttons. When my children relive their hurts in the form of a dream, I don't hesitate to ask the Lord to help me meet them in that place.

When they relive their pains in brazenly obnoxious ways, prayer is not the first thought in my mind. Instead, it shifts immediately into defensive mode. With my mind ready to do battle, I am no more living from a place of peace than my children.

REFLECTIONS

Are you quick to jump on the warpath with your children? Will you ask the Lord of peace to usher your family into a place of calm, trusting him to provide all that you need?

PRAYER:

Prince of peace, I bring you my children who are lacking a sense of peace and security. They are drawn instinctively to their worry and fear. I long to demonstrate, through my actions, that true peaceful security is found in you alone. Instead, my worries and fears prevent me—and ultimately them—from knowing the confidence that is found in you. Teach me to walk in faith so that I might demonstrate the freedom from worry and fear that is found in you through Christ. Amen.

THE CRIES OF YOUR HEART:

_____

_____

_____

_____

_____

_____

_____

_____

LOOK NO FURTHER

My sheep hear my voice, I know them,
and they follow me.
—John 10:27

IT WAS A PERFECTLY beautiful summer day. The sun was warm, the breeze was gentle. Geese, cranes, and other wetland creatures were singing praises to the Lord. We had just moved into our "new to us" home, but we had been together as a family for a little over two years. We found a quiet neighborhood away from the roar of heavy traffic. The view from my upstairs windows allowed me to see the entire area, which meant I felt more confident in letting my kids play and explore.

My heart was satisfied and grateful. After taking a peek to make sure all was well outside, I turned to the mound of boxes waiting to be unpacked. Suddenly I heard a piercing cry of pain followed by gut-wrenching sobs.

As I met my middle Miss at the front door, I could see that she had scraped her knee and had a pretty decent road rash the length of her leg. Choking back the tears as best as she could, she said, "Mommy, I crashed my bike and hurt my leg!" I scooped her up immediately and sped through the house, making silly ambulance sounds until I "parked" her on my bathroom counter.

While cleaning and bandaging her wounds, I talked her through every step of the process and explained why. I told her how glad I was that she came to me and gave me a chance to help her. I told her I'd always help her, no matter what. I told her my job as her Mommy was to make sure she always felt like she could ask for help. She hobbled outside on a stiff little limp that miraculously went away in only a few minutes.

Then I cried. I cried hard and fell to my knees, thanking God for those moments with my sweet girl. After all this time of being together, this was the first time my middle Miss came to *me* instead of to her big brother. She was taking a risk, and I could have easily ignored her. I could have minimized the injury and her pain.

How could she be sure what I would do? She couldn't. All she could do was try. It was a significant growth point for all three of my kids. They each started taking more risks in coming to Daddy or me for their "boo-boos."

Most children have no problem asking Mom or Dad for bandages, and "ow-ie kisses." But kids from trauma look to each other. Sometimes it seems as if they are all functioning with one shared brain. For these kids, a lifetime has already passed, and the only consistent thing remaining is the presence of each other. So naturally, they turn to one another first.

That day was a breakthrough, and I felt honored to be included. And now I work very hard to take every request for help seriously. After all, I want them to learn to look to *me*, so they can see me look to *Jesus*.

Do your kiddos suffer from what is known as a "trauma bond?" Do you see them functioning as one rather unhealthy unit, struggling to understand why they can't yet allow themselves to be individuals? I do. I often must stop myself from trying to fix what seems broken by telling them how it should be. They don't understand. Their reality has proved they need each other.

...allow Jesus to help you to help them bond with Him.

REFLECTIONS

Let's agree to pray together that we can lay aside our propensity to attempt to break their bond. And instead, allow Jesus to help *you* to help *them* bond with him.

PRAYER:

Leader Father, the wounds my children carry are not a hindrance to you in any way. It can be easy to remain focused on the bandages rather than on the healing. I ask and believe that you will show them that there is nothing you cannot heal. Help me teach them to know your voice and give them what they need to run toward it. Amen.

THE CRIES OF YOUR HEART:

_____

_____

_____

_____

_____

_____

_____

_____

THE 50:20 PRINCIPLE

*You planned evil against me; God planned it for good
to bring about the present result—the survival
of many people.*
—Genesis 50:20

AS A MARATHON RUNNER, what has kept me going throughout a race, and apart from the Lord, is the knowledge that my family would be waiting for me at each mile marker to ring their bells and cheer me onward. Once at mile marker 23, my husband encouraged our middle daughter to run those last three grueling miles with me. She is a phenomenal cheerleader, maybe even a future preacher:

"You can do this, Mommy. I'm so proud of you, Mommy. You are the most determined Mommy I have ever had. Jesus is running with you right now, Mommy. Do you realize if it wasn't for you adopting us, we probably wouldn't know Jesus right now?"

At the end of the marathon course, with less than a quarter of a mile to go, I was exhausted, dehydrated, fighting tears, and struggling to breathe. My family all joined hands, and together we ran across the finish line! Since that day, so many correlations between running 26.2 miles and trauma parenting have come to mind:

*You can do
this,
Mommy.*

- You can have a plan in place that correctly follows every known approach to running a marathon and still feel unprepared for the big day.

- It is easy to convince yourself that you are utterly failing at executing the proper protocol for a perfect run.

- Running a marathon can get lonely. It can feel like no one else is struggling because everyone is in better condition.

- You ask yourself more than once why exactly you thought running a marathon was ever a good idea.

- When you want to quit and go home at mile 18, you keep going because you love your kids and want them to know you'll never give up on them no matter how hard things get.

- You pay too much attention to tiny twinges of pain or soreness because you believe it is the only way to protect yourself from more profound and lasting pain.

- Somehow you believe it will be worth the pain, hard work, and tears to know you did your absolute best.

REFLECTIONS

When parenting hurting kids, it is easy to get mired by the evil they have endured. While encouraging them to walk in the newness of life in Christ, you are worried about how they might be shaped by their past. Your worry becomes anxiety, and no one makes the right decisions when coming from a place of fear. Ask God to turn your eyes toward him and trust him to fulfill his promises.

PRAYER:

God Almighty, everything that is meant to serve evil, can be turned around to serve good. My children have already endured incredibly difficult times. They have experienced devastating loss and believe that nothing ever has or ever will go their way. I ask you to help them see that you can turn their loss into something useful. If it would please you, would you redeem the evil they have endured to build unshakable faith? Only by your grace, Lord, can this be so. Amen.

THE CRIES OF YOUR HEART:

_____

_____

_____

_____

_____

_____

_____

_____

THE NEIGHBORS' GRASS
IS GREENER!

Therefore, let us approach the throne of grace with boldness, so that we may receive mercy and find grace to help us in time of need.
— Hebrews 4:16

IT'S SUNDAY MORNING. You've given up on expecting to arrive on time for church. These days you're just glad when your entire family actually makes it to church. As you attempt to settle into a row of seats without creating too much distraction, you notice the lights are dimmed. It's worship time. Heads are bowed, eyes are closed. Voices and hands are raised up to the heavens.

The tween girl in front of you leans into her dad, who gently squeezes her against him in a side hug. Her brother is on the other end. He's a little older, a little taller, and has one arm wrapped around his mom's shoulder while the other is raised up in a gesture of receiving.

It's beautiful and even brings a small tear to your eye. Longing for the same connection with your children, you reach your arm gently and cautiously around the shoulders of your tween girl. She freezes, and you return your arm to your side. You fight to hold yourself together because you don't want to make a scene. But the tears are burning your eyes in a desperate plea to escape.

When it's time to be seated, you catch a glimpse of your husband lifting his arm to rest it on the back of your son's seat, an attempt at closeness without physical contact. You observe your son slowly lean forward and rest his elbows on his knees to create distance from that all-invasive arm. You close your eyes and swallow hard.

After the service, your children quickly head for the cookies. Along the way, you watch them stop and embrace "Mrs. So-and-So" who teaches Sunday School. Your daughter gladly receives a loving embrace from the mother of her friend. As your heart sinks even lower, you wonder if you'll ever have a chance to be as close to your children as the others. You wonder what you're doing wrong to make them seemingly repelled by you.

But once again, you hear the words shared ever-present in your adoptive moms' support group, "It's not personal." However, it sure feels personal. So, you put on your plastic smile, push the hurt down into your stomach, and press on. What else can you do?

While our hurting kids are not rejecting us out of hatred but rather out of fear, indeed rejection still feels like rejection. It stings! Our kids are persistently in survival mode. Although we are the safest and most reliable people in their lives, we represent the potential for more pain and sorrow.

> *Our kids are persistently in survival mode.*

REFLECTIONS

This may not be the way you imagined it would be. But comparing your relationship with your kids against the dynamics of any other family is unfair to your kids and unfair to you. Your value is not measured in how much you physically embrace your kids.

PRAYER:

Loving God, you are all that I need. You give so much good that I often fail to notice. I am easily distracted from true contentment and find myself longing for a different life. Parenting children from trauma is sometimes taxing and tiresome. Help me lay aside my expectations for a perfect family. Teach me to be as generous as you in mercy, grace, and love. Let my family represent you and all that you have given with honor. Amen.

THE CRIES OF YOUR HEART:

_____

_____

_____

_____

_____

_____

_____

_____

_____

BEAUTY TRULY *IS* IN THE EYE OF THE BEHOLDER

♥

...to provide for those who mourn in Zion; to give them a crown of beauty instead of ashes, festive oil instead of mourning, and splendid clothes instead of despair. And they will be called righteous trees, planted by the Lord to glorify him.
—Isaiah 61:3

EVERYONE IN MY HOUSEHOLD knows better than to stand between me and my first mug of coffee. We have a system. First, mom says good morning to each child and gives out hugs, next the water goes into the kettle and onto the stove to come to an almost boil: 218° not 220°. While the water is heating, fresh Italian roast coffee beans are ground in a hand grinder and poured into the stainless-steel French press.

The sound water makes in a tea kettle, once it reaches the proper temperature, is etched in my auditory memory. When that sound occurs, I pour the hot water into the press, stir, and wait precisely four minutes. With a wooden spoon, the top crust of beans is scooped off the top of the liquid and deposited in a container for later use in the garden.

The coffee is now ready. All that's left is to press the plunger, pour the liquid heaven into a mug and top it off with half and half. One or two sips and I am ready and able to converse. Ideally, the entire process is worked from beginning to end before anyone except Jack Sparrow, our rooster, is awake for the day!

Sometimes mornings come way too early. I forget to turn on the burner of the stove, one of more kid has a thousand questions that must be answered NOW, and the brief window between 217° and 220° is gone in a flash. Besides, there is one member of our household who doesn't seem to care if she gets in the way of this perfectly honed routine.

She often follows me close, sticking her cold, wet nose on my bare leg. As I stand there grinding beans, she will sit down behind me, watching my every move. And when I turn to walk toward the stove, I trip and stumble, trying to stop myself from landing on her.

"Kyla!" I say. "You have to stay out of the way, sweet dog; I don't want to squash you."

Her ears sag, and she drags her lowered tail into the other room. We have decided she must keep a watchful eye in case I accidentally drop something for her to clean up. Eventually, I sit in the recliner, laying my Bible in my lap, while thanking God for another day of waking up alive, drinking in my coffee and His word. My husband has given up on trying to drink my pristine taste of glory.

"That stuff could melt a horseshoe!" He's sweet, I love him!

I share this morning routine for a few reasons. One, my son suggested it, and I love that my kids want to be involved in this project. The second is because I think every adoptive mom should know how to brew a perfect cup of coffee. Truly.

The third reason also involves my son. He said that the lesson we should all learn is that in life, we try and try. And we get tripped up, try again, and trip yet again. We may not always get what we want, but we should never stop striving for the things we think are good. Coming from a thirteen-year-old boy, who has seen more pain than many adults, that's fairly profound. The most powerful lesson in this, for me, was my son's honest perspective.

> *We may not always get what we want, but we should never stop striving for the things we think are good.*

REFLECTIONS

It is super easy, even natural for us mommas to get so bogged down by the weight of our kids' attempts to manage their grief, that we forget to notice they are living, breathing, growing, and developing human beings who need direction along the path. I often pray for God to help me see things from his whole perspective. Will you pray along with me?

PRAYER:

God and Father, my heart desires to see my children choose to walk in purity. If only I could erase all the horror they have experienced. I cannot, but your word promises beauty is made from ashes. As I wait for that beauty to be realized by my precious ones, help me teach them to focus on whatever is: true, honorable, just, pure, lovely, commendable, excellent, and praiseworthy. I pray for my children to learn to see themselves from your perspective. Help me to also see myself through your eyes. Amen.

THE CRIES OF YOUR HEART:

_____

_____

_____

_____

_____

_____

_____

_____

WHO JUST SAID THAT?

Look, God shows himself exalted by his power. Who is a teacher like him?
—Job 36:22

EVERY LAST PIECE of the enormous stack of adoption paperwork had been filled out, submitted, reviewed, and approved. In the eyes of the State of Michigan, my husband and I were fit to adopt their wards. We were left with the hefty task of waiting. Having already walked through infertility and loss, we were anxious to build our family utilizing the path God had laid out before us. Nightly we shared the practice of praying for God to prepare our hearts for whomever He sent and to prepare the hearts of the children who would only become ours by suffering a significant loss.

We shared images in our minds of two little girls, close in age, enjoying pink princess bedrooms and stuffed animal tea parties. After what seemed like forever, we were invited to adopt a group of three siblings under the age of 8. Although not quite what we had imagined, we were confident that the Lord had perfectly arranged the combination of parents who longed for children and children who wanted for a forever home. No doubts.

Our son and his two sisters became ours to raise and love. Once we were joined as a family and living under the same roof, it became natural for me, having been in ministry, to facilitate conversations about the Lord with our kiddos. It was during one such discussion that my deep-thinking son asked a compelling question.

"Mom, how did you know that we were the kids God wanted you to have?"

I told him our story about how we imagined adopting two girls, but that God had a better plan. Being transparent in sharing that we were nervous when we heard three kids needed a forever home, rather than two, I told him, "One evening I was looking at my email, and a picture of you guys came through from the social worker. I turned the screen around to Dad and said, 'These are our kids, I just know it.' Dad agreed. The very next day, we responded to the email confirming our intent to adopt you."

...how did you know that we were the kids God wanted you to have?

Unfortunately, what my son heard was this, "We only wanted girls, but there were no girls to adopt, so we agreed to take you so that we could get your sisters."

At least five years have passed since that conversation, and our son still believes his version is the correct account of what took place. We have cried together and prayed about it. We have retold the story together again, and again, and again.

Still, our son sees himself as an inconvenience, a means to an end. When he has a need, he often doesn't ask. If he is injured, he either amplifies the minor wounds or minimizes the severe injuries. In the face of correction and discipline, he is reduced to tearful anxiety because he holds such great fear and trepidation for the day when we have had enough of him and decide to send him away.

It has taken much time, but I have finally come to a place of recognizing that he believes this lie so extensively only the Master Teacher can bring him to a place of Truth. My only option is to pray for him, and to model a life lived from a place of confident rest in the One who is Truth.

REFLECTIONS

Are you resting in Truth? Join me in asking God to open our hearts to his voice alone.

PRAYER:

Teacher God, there are so very many voices vying for our attention. It can be challenging to discern what comes from you and what comes from Satan. Teach me to listen carefully and hear your words clearly. Use me as a minister and model for my children to develop such a hunger for your voice that all other voices are turned away. Help them whenever they must choose your way or the way that leads to destruction. Amen.

THE CRIES OF YOUR HEART:

_____

_____

_____

_____

_____

_____

_____

_____

SOMEONE GRAB A FLASHLIGHT!

Your word is a lamp for my feet
and a light on my path.
−Psalm 119:105

CONSIDERING HOW FAR she had come since she first joined our family, my heart was warmed despite the chilly temperatures. It was the last track meet of the season. Runners were shivering at the starting line, waiting until the last moment to shed their jackets. At eight years old, with a glimmer of delight in those engaging blue eyes, she beamed at the chance to line up with her friends for one last race.

Muffled instructions came through large portable speakers, then the pistol fired, and they were off. Through the wave of runners, I could see my sweet girl leading the way. She's a fast runner who enjoys every moment of every race, no matter when she finishes. She would win for sure.

Instead, she did something quite surprising. My sweet champ realized her friend was struggling to try and break free from a tight group of runners and was falling behind, so she turned around and went back for her. The two girls locked hands and broke through together.

Tears slipped down my face at the opportunity to see my daughter care more about her friend than about the finish line. Once they were over the hill, I could only wait and watch. When runners started coming in, I struggled to find my daughter and her friend. The count off began, "*Here comes our number one runner...runner number twelve, thirteen...*"

At last, I saw them, no longer holding hands but still side by side and wearing giant grins; they were having fun. My daughter finished at the bottom of the top 20, slowing at the end so her friend could finish in 19th place. She wore her medal the remainder of the day, along with her big smile.

Too many times...I fear that I will not succeed.

Too many times, I get myself stuck on the difficulties of parenting kids from trauma. I think about the tantrums, the bruises on my legs, the bite marks hidden under my sleeves, and I fear that I will not succeed. How well am I doing in preparing them to participate in adult society?

REFLECTIONS

What about you? Do you get bogged down by tantrum after tantrum until you are so anxious about the next tantrum you miss the in-between moments? Pray with me that we would learn to see the things upon which God is shining his light rather than focusing on the darkness. It's time to take notice of how they are engaged in life now.

PRAYER:

Author of life, it is written that your word is a lamp for our feet and a light for our path. Even knowing this, I walk in trepidation and fear as if at any moment you might extinguish the light and leave me to find my way through the dark places. Remind me often of my security in you. Use me to demonstrate to my children, who once lived in nothing but uncertainty, that you are always holding us. Give them the courage they need to be able to step surefooted along your path for them. Amen.

THE CRIES OF YOUR HEART:

_____

_____

_____

_____

_____

_____

_____

_____

_____

YOU CAN'T PLEASE EVERYONE

I am at rest in God alone; my salvation comes from him. He alone is my rock and my salvation, my stronghold; I will never be shaken.
−Psalm 62:1-2

YOU SIT THROUGH hours of training, giving up your Saturday morning sleep in to attend state-mandated education. The professionals go on and on about the effects of trauma on a young developing brain, but you only half-listen while thinking, *"These kids just need someone to love them, and I've got plenty of love to give."*

Concepts like the significance of "trauma brain" and "trauma bonds" are merely abstract while you doodle hearts on the back of the infographic handout. The term "emotional age" keeps coming up, and you aren't sure why it matters.

"I'll love them. No matter what, I'll raise these children on the love of Christ."

When a match is found, you receive photos of cherubic children who are cute and sweet. Adoption Day at the courthouse is the fulfillment of your dreams as the judge declares what you already know in your heart−you are a family. Relatives and friends all applaud and embrace you for rescuing these lucky children.

Everything is perfect, and you think that nothing could bring you down. "*I've got this,*" continually runs through your mind!

Your new family works together to bond, establish traditions, and lay ground rules, while you pour out as much love and grace as possible. Maybe you notice some resistance to your affections, but you tell yourself, "*They just need time, when they see how much I love them, they'll come around.*"

On occasion, your kids are the picture of absolute perfection and charm outside of the walls your call home.

After all, you love them and always will. Only too soon, it becomes clear that you can no longer dismiss the increasing occurrences of lying. There are food wrappers stashed in the laundry, urine is sprayed on the closet floor, and feces are spread on the walls. You berate yourself when you lose your patience and swear to God, you will love them better.

But there's more lying. More sneaking. More mess. Exhaustion sets in, and you cry yourself to sleep most nights. Sometimes your kids act wild and crazy in public, and you try to not notice the judgmental looks, snorts, and comments about how someone should control those children.

On occasion, your kids are the picture of absolute perfection and charm outside of the walls you call home. Growing fatigued from having to explain and justify your every thought and action in your parenting, you stop sharing. You stay home more and interact less. Friends who were "tight" fall away when you don't comply with their solutions. Loneliness sets in. Eventually, you just hide in your room because the thought of feeling like a failure for even one more afternoon is unbearable.

REFLECTIONS

Are you tired? Feeling defeated? Do you feel guilty for not following through on all you've read about connecting with your hurting kids? Good. When it comes to the perils of this world—including what has happened to our children, real rest comes in the letting go, not in giving-up. And it comes in rising-up with renewed strength that comes only from our Lord. Is it time for you to loosen your grip and pray?

PRAYER:

Sweet, loving, and patient Father, at some point in life, we all have fallen into the trap of believing we only have value and security when we have utterly pleased those around us. My children, who are from hard places, consider this to the core of their being. They either fall into a false persona of pleasing others with no regard for their own wellbeing, or they feel such inability to please anyone, they go out of their way to show that they are not going to try. I implore you to meet me in the places I do not see you and use me to turn my children's eyes toward you. Amen.

THE CRIES OF YOUR HEART:

_____

_____

_____

_____

_____

_____

_____

_____

HONEST TO GOODNESS!

The One who lives with integrity lives securely, but whoever perverts his ways will be found out.
−Proverbs 10:9

I THINK IT MIGHT have been the hottest summer on record in Michigan. We had just settled into our new home. At the time, it seemed reasonable to host a cookout for the people in our Sunday school class, along with all their children. There was every type of picnic food imaginable, ice-cold drinks, games for the children, and a big bad Dad grill. As usual, I had a kind of movie script playing in the back of my mind that represented how things were supposed to go that day. So far, things were spot on.

My son came to me with a small square pouch filled with sand and pointed to a small hole in one of the seams. I made a passing comment about how it was nothing to worry about. Knowing that it could be easily repaired, I asked him to put it on the kitchen counter and then forgot all about it.

Later, grease in the grill caught fire and ignited the dry grass, but it was quickly soaked down with the garden hose until it was nothing but mud. Everyone packed up their own chairs and dishes, grabbed their tired, sunburned kids, and headed for air-conditioned homes. It had been a long, harrowing day, and I was ready to collapse onto the couch and wait for winter to come.

Upon entering the kitchen, I spotted the little red sandbag my son had shown me earlier. The bag was now mostly empty. Puzzled, I walked toward the counter to investigate and found that there was sand everywhere! There was sand in my cookbooks, in some home school materials, and all over the counter.

I turned to my son, who had just entered the kitchen, and I asked what happened. He told me he put the sandbag on the counter like I had asked.

"How did the sand get all over the place then?" I asked.

> *I realize I was stuck on my own lie.*

"I'm not sure." He replied coolly. "Maybe it exploded." And then here's how the conversation went:

"Are you sure you didn't toss it over here because you wanted to hurry, and it hit the wall spilling its contents?"

This was followed by, "No, I walked in and set it down like you told me."

At this point, I should have let it go. Instead, I dug in for more. I knew my son was not telling the truth. He knew he was not telling the truth. And I was determined for him to admit he lied. And he was determined to repeat the lie over and over again.

I'm not sure what I was thinking at that moment but, when I look back now, I realize I was stuck on my own lie. My son had lied. Somehow, in those moments, I had decided that if I didn't get the truth, I was failing. Here's a hint. He never wavered from his original story.

REFLECTIONS

I'm learning that it is so essential to remember who I truly am in Christ to survive this call God has given me. If I am in Christ, I can operate from a place of emotional rest in him. When my emotions aren't ramped up with my own lie-based thinking, my son's faults are not my failures. It's a tough thing to remember in the thick of it, but I'm working on it. Will you join me?

PRAYER:

Lord of everything, my desire is that you would move in my children's hearts. Help them to be open to guidance along a path toward honesty, integrity, and hope to be like Jesus. You have taught us, through your Proverbs, that those who live with integrity will live securely. Everyone hopes to feel secure, especially our kids from hard places. Give us the courage we need to dwell within your security. Amen.

THE CRIES OF YOUR HEART:

_____

_____

_____

_____

_____

_____

_____

_____

_____

FIRST THINGS FIRST

*But seek first the kingdom of God and his
righteousness, and all these things
will be provided for you.*
—Matthew 6:33

"MOM, IF YOU get me in-line skates for my birthday,
I won't ask for anything else." He used them for about
two weeks!

"I'd like to get a really nice mountain bike and go to
a mountain bike camp this summer. There is nothing
I want to do more." And so, it goes.

Our son wants everything he sees: the gaming
systems, the sporting equipment, the smartphones,
the branded clothing, the celebrity shoes. Like so
many others, adults included, my son's underlying
agenda is about filling emotional holes.

As you would expect, my expressed concerns to
friends and family are answered with, "All kids do
that." I agree with one reservation.

The thoughts and actions of kids from hard
beginnings are rooted in fear. My son seems to be
attempting to recreate what he believes he lost when
removed from his original home. "Before we were
tooken away, my dad made a theater in our
basement."

It is much easier to reflect on fun things, rather
than those that are frightening. When asking the

Lord for direction on how to help my sweet boy with this issue, I heard more about me than about him. Sometimes mommas, adoptive or not, try to fill emotional holes with perfection. If I could just figure out how to respond rather than react...If I could allow the Lord to shut my mouth—If I could—then I'd be a good mother.

Self-sufficiency is so very insufficient. Why fill the water jug with murky water when there is a clear stream up ahead? We know our children pay more attention to what we *do* than to what we *say*. If my son watches me be utterly dissatisfied with life because something didn't go my way, what has he learned? Emotional holes are only sufficiently filled by Christ. Anything else will never work.

Self-sufficiency is so very insufficient.

Our sinful nature draws our focus to anything that will distract us from Jesus and the life he brings. Mommas, we can spend a whole lot of time and energy seeking perfection in our parenting and never truly parent well without first seeking Jesus.

REFLECTIONS

Hurting kiddos are fighting with all their might against the fear and emptiness left by trauma. It's time we stop telling them what won't work and start showing them what will work.

PRAYER:

Perfectly loving Father, your Holy Word challenges us to seek first your kingdom and righteousness. Instead, I am so easily enticed by the priorities of this world. I forget perfection exists in Christ alone. My children experience such an empty and gnawing hunger to feel safe, loved, and accepted. They quickly feed on what the world says they need. I humbly ask that, through your loving kindness, I would learn and model for my family the fulness that comes in seeking you above all else. Amen.

THE CRIES OF YOUR HEART:

_____

_____

_____

_____

_____

_____

_____

_____

FOLLOW THE LEADER

*He renews my life; he leads me along the right paths
for his name's sake.*
−Psalm 23:3

HOW MOTHERS PURSUE *Jesus has a lasting effect on our
children.* It has been a few years since our pastor spoke
those words into the hearts and minds of our church
family. Since we usually skip Mother's Day, I don't recall
why we were even there. But the notes in my journal
stand as proof.

The longer I am a mother, the more I see the power of
that truth. My momma has already left this earth and her
broken-down body to be with Jesus, her precious savior.
She wasn't perfect, but my momma had an ever so sweet
relationship with the Lord. My dad once shared that her
final exhale on this earth was used to cry out the name
of Jesus.

Memories of my momma still echo peacefully through
my thoughts nearly thirteen years later. My children
never met my momma. The only way for my kids to
know her is through the stories I tell and the passing
along of lessons learned. We'll bake her Wacky Cake
recipe together as I tell them about how on Thursdays
after school, we were greeted with the yeasty aroma of
fresh-baked loaves of bread mixed with the
unmistakable essence of chocolate chip cookies, cake,
or cinnamon rolls. I tell them how much she would have

loved them and spoiled them with chocolate no-bakes, or scratch-made pudding.

My momma was silly, just like me, and opinionated, also (*ahem*) like me. And she was unashamed of the gospel, which is something I work on every day. When I have a sleepless night, I usually grumble and grunt throughout the next day, frustrated that no amount of coffee can replace the sweet restoration that comes from a good night of sleep. My momma, however, refused to let the time she couldn't sleep go to waste. She figured if she wasn't sleeping, there must be something the Lord is asking her to pray about.

So, she would get up out of bed, get down on her knees, and using the mattress as her altar, she would pray. She prayed for her children, for the church, for the pastor and his family. She prayed for this world and the next-door neighbor. My momma even prayed for the televangelists!

All these amazing aspects of my momma went unappreciated while she was living...

Then she would get up and start her day reckoning that if she wasn't sleeping, she may as well cook, or sew, or talk to her houseplants (*she swore they listened to her*).

Momma had dark days too when she was so stuck on her turbulent past, she couldn't find Jesus, but I never witnessed her turning away. All these amazing aspects of my momma went unappreciated while she was living (*well, except for the chocolate part*)! I suppose I figured there would be plenty of time for that later.

Now, as a mother myself, I find that her lessons were stored like a treasure in my heart. In times of crisis, I have learned to say, "Let's stop and pray." When adoptive life gets overwhelming, and it is difficult to find the answers, I proclaim, "Keep your eyes on Jesus." My kids see me settle into the Word first thing in the morning, sometimes even before coffee! They also see me have bad days, sad days, and hard days. Later, we talk through those days and conclude, "Isn't it so great to have Jesus always with us?"

REFLECTIONS

Our kids watch our every move, especially on our dark days. They know we have days when we don't feel like being therapeutic parents and wonder if we are going to survive. They are so tuned in to us, even when they seem far off track. Knowing this makes me want to do better. And the way to do better is to turn to the Lord for provision.

PRAYER:

Leader God, no matter how hard I try to protect my children from the evil influences of this dark world, they are vulnerable every day. They suffer the sting of their own past and the fallen state of creation. I trust you to use me to teach them to be followers of you alone. Help me to train them to be leaders among their peers while they discover your transforming power. Help them see that even they can make a difference in your name. Amen.

THE CRIES OF YOUR HEART:

_____

_____

_____

_____

_____

_____

_____

_____

THE DECLARATION
OF DEPENDENCE

Humble yourselves before the Lord, and
he will exalt you.
—James 4:10

MEMORIES OF my big brother running alongside my banana seat bicycle, holding the back to keep me steady, glide through my thoughts as if forty years had not already passed.

"Keep pedaling," he instructed. Then suddenly, "Put on the brakes. The brakes. Use the breaks!" The trouble was, I didn't know what that meant.

My brother kept yelling, and my feet kept pedaling out into the street. Losing confidence as I saw the oncoming car, I stopped pedaling, fell over with my bicycle, and skidded into the path of the vehicle. The screeching of tires on asphalt still rings in my ears, and the resulting scars of road rash are still visible.

I trusted my brother implicitly, and still do. In those brief moments, my failure to use the brakes, resulting in the crash, was my fault. Even so, my big brother dusted me off, picked up my bicycle, and walked me home. Then, he made me get on the bike, showed me how to work the brakes, and we started again.

During our first summer together as a family, our kids were gifted with new bicycles. It was an exciting day. They had never owned bikes. Our middle daughter, who was six at the time, was concerned that other kids in our neighborhood did not require training wheels.

After a time, I took them off, but then she wouldn't ride. Having experienced a handful of skinned knees and scraped hands while using training wheels, she was afraid. I could relate. Determined to help her overcome fear, I offered to help her learn.

We talked about balance, turning, when to pedal and when to coast, and how to use the brakes. She was instructed to straddle the bicycle, scoot her bottom onto the seat, then take off with the help of the highest pedal. As soon as she started to pedal, I let go, and she fell. Immediately, I assumed that she was not able to trust me. So, I asked her brother to help. He tried and failed, as well. Then I thought of the neighbor girl. My daughter admired her, perhaps she could help. Nope.

Surprisingly, there was no need to hold my daughter in balance.

Soon it was the fourth of July; we had a big day visiting family and playing with cousins. Upon arriving home, I spotted the bicycle cast aside as if she had given up. I turned to my sweet girl and said, "I feel like this is the day that you are going to learn to ride your bike." She agreed reluctantly.

"This time, I am going to hold onto the seat the way my brother did for me," I told her, and off we went.

Surprisingly, there was no need to hold my daughter in balance. She was doing it on her own! I let go and simply continued to run beside her; this happened over half a dozen times.

Then without saying a word, I stood still while she took off on her own. Waiting until she reached the end of the driveway and was turning around, we all cheered, whooped and hollered.

"You're doing it! Look at you go! I knew you could do it."

And that was the key. My daughter knew how to ride a bicycle, she just didn't believe that she could. My presence said, "I believe in you even when you doubt."

REFLECTIONS

Are there opportunities in your child's life where you may need to let go? Perhaps a situation where they need your presence, but don't require you to hold on so tight?

PRAYER:

Sustainer God, absolutely no one can do anything of value apart from you. We live in a time when the pride of independence keeps us from fully discovering the rest that comes from dependence on you. Help me not only to learn but also to teach and model, for my children, an attitude of humility. Amen.

THE CRIES OF YOUR HEART:

_____

_____

_____

_____

_____

_____

_____

_____

MIRROR, MIRROR ON THE WALL

*Humans do not see what the Lord sees, for humans see
what is visible, but the Lord sees the heart.*
–Samuel 16:7b

"THANK YOU, Mom, for buying me skinny jeans,
'cause now I can be skinny." My seven-year-old
daughter expressed her gratitude while modeling
her new indigo-colored jeans.

"What do you mean?" I questioned, carefully as
always.

"A boy at recess said I'm fat, so now he can't say
that because I have skinny jeans."

My heart dropped into my stomach. I, too, was
seven years old when a boy at school named me
Beth-Tub. It was a name that would stay with me
through to High School graduation.

"Sweetheart, I didn't buy skinny jeans for you
because someone thinks you are fat. You are
beautiful just as you are because everything God
makes is beautiful."

Eyes downcast now, she mumbled her
understanding and ran off to show her sister and
brother her new outfit. It wasn't long before I heard
her proclaim to them, "Now I can be skinny!"

My poor girl. It made me angry for her sake, angry
for my sake. And I was sad for all the young boys

and girls who believe that the labels other people assign to them contain the truth about their value. Knowing that my children are also burdened with something so trite as the size of their jeans sickened me.

As a trauma momma, my heart aches daily for my children's hearts. I want so badly to restore their purity, to recover the loss of their innocence. If there was a pill I could give them or a class that would aid me in erasing their past, you could be sure I'd be first in line. I can tell my children every day that they are perfectly precious in the sight of God, but if the lies from their beginning on this earth are firmly rooted, they will struggle to decide which is true.

...they are perfectly precious in the sight of God...

My momma used to say, "Do as I say, not as I do." But that's just not reality. My kids are watching. They notice each lipstick check in the rearview mirror. They see me roll my eyes when their daddy tells me I'm beautiful. They hear the words against myself for the extra padding around my middle. They take it in and act it out.

Since that day, I have determined in my heart to be as nice to me as I am to anyone else. It's tougher than I thought it would be, so I've asked the Lord daily to lend me his perspective.

REFLECTIONS

Do you do the same thing? Do you ask your kids to love you when you don't even love yourself? Is it time for you to join me in praying for a new way to see the reflection in the mirror?

PRAYER:

Faithful Father, your word tells us that you look beyond our physical appearance straight through to our hearts. The world distracts us from that truth with a focus on the physical. I pray today that you would help me remember that because of Christ, what you see in me is beauty. Empower my children to find confidence and self-esteem in Christ, rather than in what the world has required. Remind me to remind them that if Christ is in us, we find our true identity in him. Teach my family and me to find rest in your truth. Amen.

THE CRIES OF YOUR HEART:

_____

_____

_____

_____

_____

_____

_____

_____

HE'S NOT GOING ANYWHERE

Therefore, we may boldly say, "The Lord is my helper; I
will not be afraid.
What can man do to me?"
– Hebrews 13:6

FIFTY CHICKENS share a space in Dad's Workshop turned garden shed, turned chicken coop. I just love keeping chickens. Aside from the fresh eggs that help me to provide home-cooked meals for my family, our chickens offer quite a lineup of entertainment.

When a hen finds a treat, she doesn't just gobble it quickly before another hen notices. She must first announce her find, "Bawk! A carrot peel! Squawk!"

When everyone else comes running, she grabs up her treasure and proceeds to run around the yard dodging all the other hens who now want what she has found. The show reminds me of televised sports. Sometimes the coveted item changes hands so quickly you lose track of who actually has it until they've run toward the goal.

We have a hen named Rose. She's the best chicken to have around when a person is digging into the ground. She stands at the ready and jumps in to snatch any worms, slugs, or bugs that are unearthed. Rose has learned to stay quiet, thus keeping an entire gourmet delight all to herself.

Then there's Goldie. My sweet Goldie is a Buff Orpington, she's a light tan (buff) in color and is larger-than-average in size. Goldie is special to me because she's a survivor. She's blind in one eye and has what is called a "scissor-beak." Her top and bottom beaks don't line up correctly, making it difficult to eat.

The thing I don't like about chickens is their intolerance for weakness. I have witnessed how quickly the "top hen" can direct her followers to take out the weaklings. So, I have worried over Goldie, spending extra time with her each day. Scissor-beak is difficult enough. Then add the blindness to one eye. There have been many times when she pecks at and misses a tasty morsel before another hen snatches her treat away.

For several weeks after discovering her deformity, I would check on Goldie first thing in the morning. She grew accustomed to my presence and developed into a rather tame pet-like bird. I trained her to stand on my raised forearm and give me a peck on the cheek. I gave her pep talks that included not letting the other ladies get her down. She *She's doing just fine as chickens go.* learned the sound of my voice and would come running, happily flapping to discover what I had to share.

Goldie is now three years old. Occasionally we will find her a little beaten up by her hen sisters, but for the most part, they allow her to be included with the flock. We've even observed her in a position of "top hen" from time to time. She's doing just fine as chickens go.

I suspect my kids suggested a story about Goldie because she represents hope. In the world of chicken keeping, scissor-beak is often a cause for the destruction of the bird. Knowing the nature of chickens and the potential abuse she could endure, we have instead given Goldie a fighting chance by helping her get the nourishment she needs to grow strong.

REFLECTIONS

Often, kids from traumatic beginnings struggle to know who is considered a safe person. They may *trust* someone dangerous and *distrust* someone who is safe. Without guidance, they are vulnerable to any kind of depravity. We can't change their past, but with our eyes on the Lord, we can trust him with their future.

PRAYER:

Caring Father, I ask that you surround my children with friendships and relationships that always point them to you. Guard them against those with wrong motives. Strengthen their tender hearts and lives to stand against evil influences. Help them to know and believe that you are always with us and will never abandon any of us. Amen.

THE CRIES OF YOUR HEART:

_____

_____

_____

_____

_____

_____

_____

_____

THEY SAY THAT CONFESSION IS GOOD FOR THE SOUL

♥

*If we confess our sins, he is faithful and righteous to
forgive us our sins and to cleanse us
from all unrighteousness.*
−1 John 1:9

SNAKES, TOADS, FROGS, and salamanders OH
MY! Our neighborhood is planted on an area of dry
ground in the middle of some wetlands. It's beautiful
here, and I thank God every day for providing it.

Although living in a wetland area means no leaf
raking in the fall (*yay*), it does mean that our yard and
fields are sometimes overrun with creepy-crawly
critters. Somewhat relieved that our son is not terribly
interested in capturing critters and showing them off
to me, we have an understanding. If he sees Dad
heading toward the house with a surprise for me,
please try to warn me. Still, the love of my life believes
he should bring me all the cute things he captures!

On one occasion, he snatched up a rather giant toad,
excited he brought it into the house for Linus, one of
our four black cats. Linus laid, legs curled under, and
waited for the thing to move. When Mr. Toad didn't
move, Linus leaned in for a sniff. Still no movement.
He leaned in farther and made a long swipe with his
tongue up the toad's back.

What ensued was a comical frenzy as Linus desperately tried to wipe the horrid taste from his tongue. He rubbed at his mouth with his front paw. When that didn't work, Linus began licking the carpet. Crouching low to the floor, the poor cat finally scurried to the water dish where he drank deeply. The toad never moved, and you can be sure that to this day, Linus is much more cautious about friends brought home by Dad.

When my daughter suggested this story, I suspected it was because it is a fun, memorable story. I asked, "Okay, but what would you say is the lesson we could learn from it?"

Our sin tastes bad to God.

Her profound response was, "Our sin tastes bad to God."

Sin does indeed leave a terrible taste in God's mouth. Y'all, this girl is eight! She struggles with severe dyslexia, overwhelming anxiety, and earth-shaking tantrums. I must confess that until now, I have underestimated her level of understanding and God's ability to overcome absolutely everything.

My focus has been on borrowing trouble from the future. How will she ever get caught up in school? Will she learn to manage anxiety? What if she still throws tantrums when she is older? And just like that—insert finger-snapping—God showed me her heart, the place he looks while the rest of us worry.

REFLECTIONS

Trauma mommas, most days, it feels like we're raising our kids while standing in a patch of quicksand. No matter how hard we work, pray, lecture, yell, cry, beg...it still feels like we are sinking. The trouble is that the whole time we are sinking deeper and deeper into hopelessness, the creator of the universe is extending a staff and inviting us to grab hold. Admittedly, some days I don't want to. I'd rather sink. But grabbing hold of what the Lord is offering, his life in us, can lift us up and help us see that he wasn't mistaken when he asked us to mother his most vulnerable treasures. He always knew we could do it.

PRAYER:

Redeemer God help me teach my children to be quick to confess their sins. Soften their hearts and mine, with an overwhelming desire to make right what we have done wrong. I pray that, through you, I will be able to usher them from a place of shame and condemnation to a place of living in the freedom and wisdom that comes with forgiveness. Amen

THE CRIES OF YOUR HEART:

_____

_____

_____

_____

_____

_____

_____

_____

HANDS-ON EXPERIENCE

*Heal me, Lord, and I will be healed; save me, and I will
be saved, for you are my praise.*
–Jeremiah 17:14

MY SIMMERING TEMPER had come to a full boil. If I
didn't release the pressure soon, I would likely, as my
mother would say, "blow a gasket." Knowing that my
daughter had managed to push every button on my very
last nerve in about two minutes flat, I disappeared to my
bedroom to vent to my sister via text messaging.

Praise the Lord for text messaging. I could spew out
my frustration with my thumbs and avoid the risk of a
child overhearing. "You are not going to believe what she
just did!" My thumbs slid over the screen at
unimaginable speed as I typed out my story.

It was long. So long, in fact, that my cell service split it
up into three separate text messages. I took a deep
breath as I waited for my sister's response. My phone
chimed, and the screen lit up, "She's you." That was all.

"No," I typed, "this is different..." explaining all the
reasons why I should feel justified in my fierce battle
with my daughter. Send, breathe, wait, breathe, chime.

"She's you." What was going on here? Did someone
steal my sister's cell phone? She's a social worker for
heaven's sake and would never say such a thing! I've
literally known her my whole life. We grew up together,

attended the same college, became roommates after graduation. My sister, my bestie.

"Who is this?" I questioned, adding a confusion emoji.

"The reason she gets you so upset is that she is just like you. Everything you don't like about yourself and see in her makes you angry." (Actually, she used a much stronger wording than angry, but this is a Christian book!)

What? How could she say that? This is my sister. I know everything about her. She knows everything about me and—oh. There it was!

My sister didn't give me the go-ahead to stay angry with my daughter. She didn't soothe my ego and offer a sympathetic reminder about how kids from trauma have a sort of radar that finds your weak spots and presses them, very, very often. No. Not my sister.

> *She loves me enough to speak the truth.*

She's my lifelong friend. She loves me enough to speak the truth. I was allowing my lie-based thinking, my beliefs about what makes me weak, or strong, valued, or worthless, to rule my relationship with my daughter. Nothing good could come of it.

"Ugh!" I wrote. "Why does it always have to be about me?"

Her response, "LOL."

I silenced my phone, buried my face in my pillow, and started to pray. I asked the Lord to calm my temper, to clear my thinking, and to speak truth into the lie I believed that had started this whole thing in the first place. Slowly, my ears stopped ringing, my breathing settled, and my steamy temper released in a calming exhale. Biology aside, my daughter *is* like me. My goal is to make sure that statement is always a compliment.

REFLECTIONS

Do your kids sometimes trigger you? Do you feel like their undying objective is to see how long it takes for your head to explode so that they can be justified in their claim that you are unfair, or don't get it, or... consider the possibility that your own wounds and lies are bubbling up and preventing you from seeing clearly. If you don't like how you respond in such moments, ask the Lord to help you discern his truth about you. Imagine how parenting from a position of truth could look.

PRAYER:

Abba, the hearts of my children are so filled with incredible pain they have endured too early in life. I ask that you give them eyes to see things from your perspective. Teach them to receive your healing touch. Grow in them such a compassion for others who are hurting that they can't help but impart your loving kindness. Amen.

THE CRIES OF YOUR HEART:

_____

_____

_____

_____

_____

_____

_____

_____

TIME TO GET DRESSED

Haven't I commanded you: be strong and courageous?
Do not be afraid or discouraged, for the Lord your God
is with you wherever you go
–Joshua 1:9

MY SON, who was almost 13 at the time, walked into the room wearing a pair of black basketball shorts. "Mom, I'm going out to play basketball for a while."

Looking up from my project to smile at him, I suddenly said, "Wait, where did those shorts come from?" I didn't remember purchasing them, but sometimes our neighbor passed along clothes to him as her older son outgrew them, so I expected his answer to confirm that the shorts came from her.

Instead, he said, "These are the ones I was wearing when I moved in. They finally fit me!"

Speechless and a little saddened, I smiled, now remembering those shorts, as he rushed out the door. When our kids first moved in with us, my son was seven years old. We have a photograph commemorating the day we picked them up from their foster family and brought them into their forever home. In that photo, he looks like he was wearing a skirt, as the too-big shorts nearly reached his ankles. The jersey he wore that day was also too baggy, along with shoes large enough for a high school boy.

I cringe at the memories of those early days of unpacking, sorting, cleaning, and tossing. Our son was not the only child of the three to own ill-fitting clothes; both girls had clothing far too large and "mature" for a six- and three-year-old. When children are abruptly removed from their biological family, and often shuffled to various foster homes, it is unusual for them to have very many things they care to call their own.

Not wanting to add to that, on the day they moved in, I gave them each a bin and said, "These will be your growing bins. Once you grow and these things fit you better, you'll have them available."

It seemed like a fair compromise but certainly did not bring an end to the struggle. For years we've battled our son over his clothing. During the first seven years of his life, his clothes were loose, so when I purchase properly fitting clothes, he complains that everything is too tight. When trying on shoes in the store, he becomes so afraid of not getting shoes that he will claim they fit even if they are falling off his feet.

He believes that his needs are an inconvenience to us...

He has adjusted some over the years, but the poor boy still gets overcome with anxiety if he needs new jeans or athletic socks, and the need for shoes brings him to tears. He believes that his needs are an inconvenience to us and must, therefore, be kept to a minimum. I try to notice and anticipate the needs of all three kids, so they don't have to worry about asking, but like any human being, I don't always get it right.

It occurs to me as I watch my children grow and mature, that their struggles are not much different than mine. I tend to believe that my needs are an inconvenience to God and that my wants—well, my wants should not ever cross my mind.

REFLECTIONS

We all bring forward lies from our past and apply them as truth to the present. When we do that, we rob ourselves of the strength and courage that comes with being clothed in God's righteousness. Will you join me in praying for the wisdom needed to show our kids to live with hope for the future, rather than with fear from the past?

PRAYER:

All-knowing God, I long for my children to be strong and courageous in you. Like you did for Joshua, empower them to be bold in standing for what is right. Help me teach them to refuse to allow the pain of their past to weaken their hope for the future. Use me to train them to clothe themselves in your armor for their protection and for your victory. Amen.

THE CRIES OF YOUR HEART:

_____

_____

_____

_____

_____

_____

_____

_____

BULLETPROOF

The Lord protects you; the Lord is a shelter right by your side.
−Psalm 121:5

WHEN SHE WAS only nine months old, our youngest, along with her four older siblings, was pried from her mother's arms and placed into the arms of a stranger. Removed from a hotbed of unimaginable violence and perversion, she and her siblings found themselves separated and planted in the unfamiliar soil of the foster care system. For the next two years, whatever female was in a place of authority became Mommy. Her foster mom was known as Grandma Mommy. During visitations, her birth mom was Mommy. As time passed, her teenage sister seemed like Mommy too.

Our sweet girl was too young to understand what was happening and too ill-equipped to ask.

By the time God brought our little miss and two of her siblings into our hearts and home, she was three years old. Her brother and sister had a basic understanding of adoption before we were joined together, but our littlest did not. Our sweet girl was too young to understand what was happening and too ill-equipped to ask.

Barely able to utter basic words, she knew just enough to call me Mommy. When she went to preschool, Miss Amy was Mommy. When she went to Sunday school, Miss Amber was Mommy. Whenever we hired a babysitter for a much-needed night away, Miss Babysitter became Mommy. My heart hurt to the point of breaking when she cried herself into hysterics because she would rather be with Mommy Miss Amy than with me. We were trained to understand that these types of behaviors were not personal, but they felt very much like rejection.

Crying out to God one exhausting afternoon, I said, "This can't continue. She has to come to understand the concept of one Mommy."

I was instructing God, of course, because he couldn't possibly know these things unless I told him! Am I right, or am I right? And just like so very many times before, he answered my prayer with a whisper that took my breath away as his Spirit made me see. I was her mommy when God said it was so, not when she said so.

When we say "yes" to God's Son, we are adopted into his family. But so often we don't understand the permanence of our position. We look to other people, things, or ideas and make them god, when our success, friendships, applause, acceptance, have in turn taken his place. Each time we make a wrong choice, we convince ourselves that this is the moment in which God will say, "Enough! I'm not your father anymore."

The beautiful part is that God knew we would put other things in his place, and still gave us the right to be his adopted children, always and forever.

REFLECTIONS

Are you able to see yourself as an adopted child of the King of the universe? It seems too impossible, doesn't it? Perhaps you can relate some of the ways to your children. They carry the weight of the trauma left by abuse, neglect, and separation, believing that no parent is going to love and care for them any better. We ask God time and again to reaffirm his love for us and our security in him; our hurting kids are asking for assurance from us.

PRAYER:

You are my shelter, God. When I am in you, no weapon raised against me will succeed. Remember your promises when it comes to my children. They are already so much more vulnerable. Please be their shield and defender. Hide them in your presence from the ways of the evil one. Protect their hurting hearts from my own human feelings as I try and often fail to love them in the way they need. Let them know with certainty that they are securely guarded on all sides. Amen.

THE CRIES OF YOUR HEART:

_____

_____

_____

_____

_____

_____

_____

_____

SOMEBODY TO LEAN ON

...for God is greater than our hearts, and
he knows all things.
—1 John 3:20b

THE EARLY AUGUST temperatures were at an all-time high for our area. Charged up with the weight of humidity and the absence of a breeze, this summer day was best enjoyed indoors. Instead, we sat on some makeshift bleachers only partially protected by the shade of an ancient maple. The air was filled with the smell of grease, popcorn, grilled meat, and the pungency of various farm animals.

Pigs were squealing. Cows were complaining. Roosters were crowing. We had to lean forward in our seats and strain our ears to hear. A few dozen participants were waiting to take a turn with the judges. In other words, it was just another day at the county fair.

My son was on standby to present his bantam hen, Tweety. I slipped from my seat and sidled over to him. "Remember what Mrs. B. said. This is your first year, and there is a huge learning curve. Don't worry about ribbons; just do your best."

He nodded nervously, and I returned to my seat. He looked so handsome. My brave boy, dressed in a white button-down shirt and black slacks, held his chicken close, and I prayed it wouldn't poop on him. Then he stepped up to take his turn. After months of raising Tweety, memorizing the biology and physiology of a chicken, and rehearsing countless practices, his presentation lasted seven minutes.

Next was the most significant challenge—waiting. Finally, after six hours, the judges had scored each student and were ready to present ribbons. I looked over at my nervous son and gave him an encouraging smile, "You did your best, and that's what counts."

He moved closer to me by millimeters until he was fully leaning into me. He wanted to do well. It didn't matter what the leader said, he hoped to place.

My heart started sagging into my stomach as I prepared myself to comfort a disappointed young boy. Beginning with the tenth place, the judges moved up the list of names. Ribbons are given to the top four. When he didn't hear his name by fifth place, his shoulders slumped a bit.

You did your best, and that's what counts.

"Now for the ribbons," the judge announced. "If I call your name, come forward and receive your prize. In fourth place we have—."

We heard his name! I cheered with delight and relief. My shocked boy looked at me with a puzzled face.

"They just said your name, buddy. Go. Go. Go!"

That ribbon now holds a place of prominence in his bedroom, along with a photo of Tweety and himself. He's wearing the biggest grin. I wish you could see it.

There are moments in this parenting adventure when we can so fully relate to our children, we know precisely what the must be thinking and feeling. There are also moments when we don't have the slightest clue what is happening behind those eyes of theirs.

REFLECTIONS

If you're like me, it's the unsure moments that get you wound up. Those are the moments when I start filling in the blanks with worst-case scenarios. I borrow trouble and add unnecessary anxiety to the moment. I'm committed to asking God for help to see more clearly when I've forgotten to depend on him; and then surrendering, again, to his wisdom. Will you join me in the surrender?

PRAYER:

Abba, sometimes mothering kids from hard places feels isolated and impossible. Help me remember that you did not just drop my children at my front door and leave me to figure out how to parent them. Nothing about them surprises you nor catches you off guard. Teach me to lean into you for the strength, knowledge, and grace I need for daily living. Amen.

THE CRIES OF YOUR HEART:

_____

_____

_____

_____

_____

_____

_____

_____

DON'T JUST CHASE THE WIND

Flee from youthful passions, and pursue righteousness,
faith, love, and peace, along with those who call on the
Lord from a pure heart.
—2 Timothy 2:22

WE WERE QUICKLY approaching a time in the year when millions of people get excited. Thanksgiving and Christmas had passed. New Year's parties were long forgotten. Grocery stores were selling out of soda pop, beer, and various snack foods. As if it is the holiday of holidays, the final football tournament of the season always holds a place of importance in households across the country.

My son, captivated by any sport you can name, was enthusiastically hopeful for a chance to see this important game. Now we are a family who doesn't *do* television. But it had become a tradition for my son and me to scour the internet for an opportunity to watch this game together. We would mute the sound during half-time and use the time to replenish drinks and snacks.

Only this year, I was about eighteen months into a *not-yet-diagnosed* chronic condition that included daily migraine headaches. No one who suffers such pain is interested in much of anything, particularly something that involves using your eyes like a televised football game. While discussing the issue with my thirteen-year-old, I apologized profusely for my physical inability to keep up with our tradition.

Yet I wasn't surprised when he calmly accepted my words. He had already set himself up long ago to curb emotion from disappointment. Then my husband suggested our son check with the neighbors. They, too, had a teenage boy and would likely be glad for our son to join.

I hesitated, long and hard. If my son was going to be watching the game without my careful eyes, who would distract him from inappropriate commercials, and a risqué half-time show? The discussion went something like this from my husband, "He will be in high school soon. He'll be exposed to all kinds of things you can't control."

My response was, "That doesn't mean we should thrust it in front of his face!"

We debated back and forth until my headache was too much, and I gave in. My husband loaded him down with snacks and sent him on his way. My final words to him were, "Have fun and make good choices."

Perhaps some of what I have been teaching that boy was sinking in after all.

He went to the neighbor's, and I went to bed. I said a little prayer about protecting his eyes and heart, then fell asleep. A while later, my cell phone vibrated with an incoming text message. Scrunching my eyes, I read, "I thought you would like to know that during half-time, your son went downstairs and played video games." My momma's heart soared with pride and relief. Perhaps some of what I have been teaching that boy was sinking in after all.

REFLECTIONS

It's true that biological parents have a genuine concern for what goes into the minds of their children. But I believe trauma mommas work extra hard to make sure that what their kids have endured way too early in life is the worst they will ever encounter. We can't always be with them, so we must trust the father who brought our children to us, that with his wisdom, we are training them well. I've started praying something like the prayer written below. Would you join me?

170

PRAYER:

God, use me and other significant influencers in my children's lives to model a life of Godly character. Give them the strength and courage to flee from what is evil and pursue what is pure. Amen.

THE CRIES OF YOUR HEART:

_____

_____

_____

_____

_____

_____

_____

_____

KNOW GOD, KNOW PEACE

*May the Lord of peace himself give you peace always in
every way. The Lord be with all of you.*
—2 Thessalonians 3:16

ARRIVING HOME from school after a frightening
walk along a high-speed city street, she reached for
the doorknob. It wouldn't turn. Being older and
stronger, her brother reached out to help but got
the same result.

It was locked. Though it wasn't the first time, nor
would it be the last, my two older children were
prevented from entering their home. On this day,
there was a new twist to the situation. They both
needed to pee! Setting their backpacks on the stoop,
they headed around to the back yard in search of
privacy.

Always the gentleman, my son stood guard while
his five-year-old sister went first. Then he fetched
her some soft leaves so she could clean herself. At
last, he took his turn behind the garage in an
overgrown thicket.

Basketball was the game of choice that afternoon
until they were finally called in for a dinner of fast
food. When I heard the story for the first time, their
tone was without malice. It seemed they were
jovially reminiscing over days gone by, oblivious to
the inappropriateness of it all.

"Well," I said, "you will never have to worry about that again. This is your *forever* home. Any time you wish to enter, the door will be unlocked. If you need to use the bathroom seven hundred times (*I always use that number. I'm not sure why?*) in one day, I'll keep it stocked with toilet paper."

The two of them exchanged a glance. Neither said a word. My sister and I have shared that same glance for over forty years, and I understand what it means. They didn't know it wasn't okay. They had been playing the part of a lookout for so long, it had continued when they moved in.

There are so many heart-wrenching stories that have come out of my children's musings. When I take time to consider them, their general lack of peace is not surprising. It's understandable when the color drains from their faces at the notion of my being upset. The blank stares that often come after experiencing correction are logical.

But regardless, fear blinds them from true peace.

The fear they had to bury not too long ago, bubbles up on its own. The slightest nuance of uncertainty or change triggers a deep-rooted alarm that perhaps they still aren't safe. It is not always that I take time to remember those things. Often, I react to a tense moment then remember later.   But regardless, fear blinds them from true peace.

REFLECTIONS

What about you? Do you need to discover or rediscover your peace in Christ? We can't train someone else how to walk in peace if we aren't already walking in it ourselves.

174

PRAYER:

Most Holy God, I know from your Word that you are the God of peace. My children so often are lacking a real sense of peace. I pray today that each child in my care would be surrounded by an unquestionable awareness of your peace. Reveal that to me peace so that I may help them to know you look on them with graciousness and love that brings everlasting peace. Amen.

THE CRIES OF YOUR HEART:

_____

_____

_____

_____

_____

_____

_____

_____

THIS BOOK IS A MUST READ

All Scripture is inspired by God and is profitable for teaching, for rebuking, for correcting, for training in righteousness.
—2 Timothy 3:16

ONE AFTERNOON my son was asking about his grandfather, my dad. My mom and dad had both passed on into glory before my children had a chance to meet them. My sweet 8-year-old asked several questions about death and dying.

I answered simply and honestly, including the fact that my father chose cremation, and my mother did not. Eventually, he realized he didn't know what the word cremation meant, so I told him.

"So, how did your dad go to heaven if his body got burned up, I thought that only happened in hell."

Surprised by the question, I answered as best as I could. Those answers led to what might be the best question that boy has ever asked me. "How do I know that I get to go to heaven?"

Assuring him that I was so glad he asked me such an important question, I silently threw up a plea for guidance from the Lord. While I was explaining through drawings the traditional Four Spiritual Laws, one of my girls entered the room. My son called her name and said, "Come look at this, Mom is going to show us how to get to heaven!"

That very evening both children chose to pray for Jesus to enter their hearts and lives. A few days after that precious moment, I took them to select their own copy of The Holy Bible. They were excited and eager to tear open the packaging and begin reading. Honestly, I figured the newness would wear off quickly when they saw the sheer volume of words. Was I in for a surprise!

The very next day, I came into the house after collecting chicken eggs and found all three children huddled together in the family room. The youngest sat between her brother and sister, each holding Bibles in their laps. They were taking turns reading a verse at a time from Genesis. Later, I told my husband that even if everything else we did parents fell flat, at least we knew that we had brought them to Jesus.

But God's word is for everyone.

I have read many excellent books about special needs adoption, therapeutic parenting, trauma brain, and the like. And it's been educational. Many of the recommendations have been effective in my parenting. Some advice has been unrealistic for our situation. I'm not going to tell you that these books are wrong or unnecessary, but I will say that there is one book through which all other books should be filtered. That book is the Word of God.

I know that it can be frustrating to go to the Word and feel like there are no answers. But God's Word is for everyone. You won't find some obscure verse hidden under a pile of platitudes about kids from trauma. What you will find, if you seek it, is the truth about who you are in Christ and how to function as a parent from that position of restful peace.

REFLECTIONS

My challenge for you this week is to ask the Lord to show you the places where you need his healing and to then bring your kids before him. Seek answers through His Word.

PRAYER:

Father, it is my prayer that my children would develop a love and desire for your Word. I want them to learn to turn to scripture for truth. Turn my own heart toward the truth written in your Word. Stir a hunger within me to seek my own healing so that I might give them insight, through the Spirit, for the wisdom and understanding that keeps their hearts tender toward you. Amen.

THE CRIES OF YOUR HEART:

_____

_____

_____

_____

_____

_____

_____

_____

FREE AT LAST!

*You will know the truth, and the truth
will set you free.*
−John 8:32

BEFORE ANYONE KNEW what was happening, she dashed out the door and down the driveway. Reaching the edge of the road, Kyla stopped, glanced back, and with tail wagging, she sprinted forward. We ran after her, calling in a very gentle tone, "Come here, Miss Kyla."

When she only darted even farther away, we tried bribing, "Here, Kyla, do you want a treat?"

The dog turned toward us and paused as if trying to decide if the treat was worth her surrender. It wasn't. By now, her trek had taken her into the wetlands behind our home. It would not be wise or safe for us to continue the chase. I cleared my throat and hollered a very firm, "Kyla, come!"

She disappeared into the marsh. By then, I was exasperated and anxious with fear.

"Kyyyyllllaaaa!"

We had been advised that chasing after her would encourage rather than discourage the behavior. It would be best to stand still and wait for Kyla to return on her own. The advice rang true as we realized that the more we chased, the more she ran as if leading her pack.

But I just couldn't do it. I couldn't stand still and do nothing. My mind was flooded with all that could happen to our canine family member. What if she got mired in the swamp? What if she got tangled in a thicket or even barbed wire? What if she ran in front of a car speeding along our country roads? What if she came face to face with a coyote? What if...I couldn't bear it.

Eventually, a neighbor who also had a dog came and stood with me. He casually asked questions about our new pet. As I answered, I felt myself calming and without flourish or flair our runaway dog appeared at my side. She was fine, filthy, but unharmed.

"Mom, why does Kyla keep running away when it's better here than where she used to be?" my son was asking.

"Well, she hasn't been with us long enough to trust that we are safe. She doesn't know that we will always make sure she has food, shelter, and lots of space to play."

She is a part of our family now.

He considered my answer. Then asked, "What if Kyla runs too far away or gets lost?"

Upon hearing my own response, I was keenly aware of his correlation between adopting him and adopting a rescue dog that keeps running off.

"She is a part of our family now. I will always do everything in my power to find her and bring her back," I advised.

It is my belief that the response God gave me for my son's question was a turning point in our relationship. Looking straight ahead, he asked, "Would you come after one of us?"

I wrapped my arm around his shoulder and replied, "Every single time."

I don't believe in coincidence because I know that it disagrees with God's nature. He never leaves us to chance, but rather orchestrates beautifully the intertwinings of our freedom in Christ and the ravages suffered in a fallen world. God knew our dog would run away, and he knew exactly how to use the event as a sort of healing balm for my son's heart. It was perfect. I wouldn't change a moment.

REFLECTIONS

Are you looking for moments when you can fortify your relationship with your kids? Are you willing to stop looking around and ask the Lord to help you see what is already there?

182

PRAYER:

Lord, I don't always feel the freedom of your promise, and sometimes I let my feelings overrule the truth, that your Spirit is always with us. I do not doubt that Christ is Truth, and I pray my children would come to know him as Savior. Help me cultivate a desire to draw near to Christ so that they can rest in his security. Amen.

THE CRIES OF YOUR HEART:

_____

_____

_____

_____

_____

_____

_____

_____

1 HAVE RIGHTS!

*But to all who did receive him, he gave them the right
to be children of God, to those who
believe in his name.*
−John 1:12

THE LIGHT in the courtroom was dim. Muted earth tones covered the walls, floor, and ceiling. The judge's bench rose in the front of the room like a high cliff too challenging to climb. A handful of family and friends squeezed into a gallery with narrow seats. The space felt almost sacred, and no one dared speak above a whisper.

We sat behind a sprawling table of dark stained hardwood. The social worker was beside us. A door I hadn't noticed opened behind the bench, and the court clerk passed through, inviting us to stand for the entering judge. My heart fluttered in my chest and butterflies in my stomach.

This was the moment! Our adoption worker would make her recommendations, and the members of the gallery would be urged to share their thoughts on the matter. When the time for affirmation ended, the judge questioned my husband and me. "Why do you think you should be allowed to adopt these children?"

I don't remember what either of us said, but I hope it was profound. Satisfied with our answers, the judge turned to our three cherubic children and asked if they had any questions. None of them spoke. He gave them a reassuring smile, picked up his gavel, and gestured toward the kids.

"There are a lot of things I get to do with this fancy robe and desk, one of my favorite things is meeting kids like you. Now, when I bang this gavel, whatever I say happens, happens." He used his gavel to point toward my husband and then toward me. "I'm about to make these two people your dad and mom. When I do, there is nothing anyone can do to change that. Do you understand me?"

BANG went the gavel! It was done. They were ours, and we were theirs. We took pictures with the judge behind his bench. Each child got to take a turn with the gavel—which is the part mu children remember most.

We left the courtroom in a kind of haze, excitement, and uncertainty mingled in the air around us. Adoption day had come and gone. We walked into the courthouse with trepidation and walked out with elation. Then we went bowling, our now annual "adoption day" tradition.

Adoption day had come and gone.

It wasn't long after that when the questions would come seemingly out of nowhere. "So, we don't have to go back to our foster family?"

I promised.

"What do you think our birth mom will do?"

I expressed her love.

Each question asked and answered again and again until the last, "Mom, if someone came and took us away from you, would you try to get us back?" What a question for an eight-year-old to carry.

"First of all," I said. "No one is ever going to take you away from us."

Not yet satisfied, "But what if someone like grabbed us and pulled us away?"

Speaking with finality, I said, "No one will EVER get you away from me. And if someone tries, I will fight like a ninja." I made a sort of karate kick to the air, and the matter was settled.

Even for adults, the world can be a lonely and frightening place if you don't know who you are or where you belong. Latching on to temporal things for identity and security can leave a person in unending turmoil as one thing after another fails to meet your needs. When you discover a relationship with Jesus and learn to settle into your identity as God's beloved child, you can finally release what is not from him.

REFLECTIONS

Do you know who you are? Have you found it to be a place of certainty? I'd love it if you joined with me in asking God to teach our weary hearts to rest in him and depend on him to guide our children.

PRAYER:

God of Love, you have such a love for us that you have given us the right to say we are your children. I pray that my children would always know just how very much they are loved, not only by me but by you. Give them the faith they need to trust that you are always faithful and true in your love for them. Teach them to find security in your love for them so that they can lower their walls and lean into you. Amen.

THE CRIES OF YOUR HEART:

FROZEN IN FEAR

For God has not given us a spirit of fear, but one of power, love, and sound judgment.
−2 Timothy 1:7

THERE IS A LITTLE GIRL living in my home who struggles quite hard to just be eight years old. She is intelligent and tenacious. When given a choice, she almost always goes for strawberry-flavored everything. She is a confident chicken keeper and dog walker. She is quiet, but when you look into her eyes, you can see that she is taking in everything thoughtfully.

What you don't see when you look into her eyes is her battle with fear. It is her constant companion. If you walk into a room catching her unaware, her startled response is so powerful it drains the color from her face.

As you might expect, I am her main concern. Since I am her primary caregiver, meaning she spends most of her days with me, it is vital to her that I am "okay" ALL THE TIME. So, she checks me. If I sigh heavily because I'm tired, her eyes snap to me. If I clear my throat, her eyes are on me. Whenever we are having a meal together, she looks at my face before taking EVERY bite.

Early on in our journey together as a family, I would become exasperated, thinking that I must be a horrible monster for my beautiful girl to believe that she must remain so vigilant. Thankfully, God gave me a husband who is not afraid to tell me to stop taking responsibility for someone else's behavior. We don't know exactly why my youngest is so fearful. What we do know is that God never intended for any child to live with such fear.

Sometimes it seems like I am backed into a corner by way of my own condemnation. The trouble is parenting is impossible from that position. It has taken a while for me to realize it is not my words or actions that bring about lasting change, it is God incarnate meeting his children in their place of fear. And that includes us, grown-up children, as well.

God never intended for any child to live with such fear.

REFLECTIONS

Do you experience self-condemning thoughts when someone has good intentions toward you? Is fear a constant companion in your parenting? Perhaps it's time to meet your heavenly Father at your point of need and allow him to show you how to parent in faith rather than fear.

PRAYER:

God, teach me to use the power of your wisdom and words. Speak your truth to me and through me in such a way that my children will learn to no longer be controlled by fear. Show them that you are bigger and stronger than any fear they feel. Help them to break free. Amen.

THE CRIES OF YOUR HEART:

_____

_____

_____

_____

_____

_____

_____

_____

I'M JUST SO WEARY

But God, who comforts the downcast, comforted us
by the arrival of Titus.
−2 Corinthians 7:6

ISOLATION was my closest friend. Relationships were a luxury. As a natural introvert, I would outwardly proclaim contentment while inward struggling with loneliness, depression, and longing for adult conversation that didn't require me to justify my parenting style. Tired of being criticized, corrected, and condemned by so-called friends who thought they knew better, I told my husband, "*I don't even want to be friends with anyone who hasn't adopted.*"

Hopelessness reigned over daily life, and tears soaked my pillow each night. My only solace, social media. But God, who remembers us even when we forget about him, used social media to connect me to a local support group for adoptive families. Desperate for a reason to get out of the house yet having zero expectations, I decided to attend one weeknight meeting.

Today I have no recollection of what was discussed in that group, but I do recall sending a text message to my husband that said, "*These are my people! They get it.*"

As if some overly muscular superhero flew in and lifted a boulder off my chest, there was unspeakable relief from breathing in the commonality and understanding. Getting out of bed in the morning became a little easier. Making mistakes in parenting brought about less self-condemnation.

Freedom and relief reign when you find you are not alone...

About a year later, a spin-off of that group was formed by three adoptive mommas who warmly welcomed me into their circle. They are "my girls." We now meet weekly at a coffee shop where we laugh, cry, celebrate progress for our kids, and pray. Freedom and relief reign when you find you are not alone in the struggle when you know you can be transparent, even vulnerable, without condemnation. I can send my girls a text message that says, "I'm not okay today." They will come back at me with prayer, truth, and love. It feels like coming home.

REFLECTIONS

Feeling isolated? Feeling like you must explain every choice and move you make as an adoptive momma? Is it time to seek the Lord for comfort like no other? He knows your darkest hurt and your deepest need. He will meet you right where you are.

PRAYER:

Thank you for your Holy Spirit, the great Comforter, who knows better than I do just what I need for each moment of each day. Hear the cry of my heart and the hearts of my children. Bring us all into a place of rest in you. Amen.

THE CRIES OF YOUR HEART:

_____

_____

_____

_____

_____

_____

_____

_____

WHERE IS THE EASY BUTTON?

Oh, Lord God! You yourself made the heavens and earth by your great power and with your outstretched arm. Nothing is too difficult for you!
–Jeremiah 32:17

THE TENSION had been building all morning. I could feel it in the air. My kids were having a bad day, and I wasn't in the mood for it. Weary and lonely from the struggle, there was a song on repeat in my head. "I can't do this anymore, it's too hard. I can't do this anymore, it's too hard, etc."

Releasing a heavy sigh, and finding some solace in scrubbing the kitchen, the words continued through my mind like an annoying song from the radio that creeps up on you throughout the rest of the day. Knowing it was just a matter of time before someone deflated our delicate bubble, I braced myself examining every nuance of every moment in hopes of being prepared. I wasn't.

During a rather firm scolding of one of my girls, the tension grew and seemed to fill the room. Suddenly, she blew up. She screamed, kicked, punched, cried, and screamed some more. I'd like to say that I remained calm until her energy was spent, but I went into panic mode.

There are so many stories in my adoptive mom support group of children who have seriously injured themselves or others when they've thrown themselves into a raging fit. All I could imagine was my little girl throwing herself through the picture window or smashing her head on the corner of a table. So, I grabbed hold and pulled her down to the floor. Her kicks and screams were only amplified.

Now she was screaming for help, and I was left realizing she didn't want my help, she wanted her brother's help. He is, after all, the chief in their trauma bond trio. Only, he stood there just as shocked as I was. He was frozen in his position at the doorway. Finally, he yelled out her name and gave the command, "Stop it!"

And she did. She gave no resistance when I pulled her toward me, rocking and whispering a prayer in her ear. Satisfied that her anger was

God, I can't keep doing this.

spent, I released her, and she went about her day as if nothing had happened. This momma went to her room and sobbed into the pillow.

"God, I can't keep doing this. It's too hard. It's too hard." Then, as usual, I replayed the incident over and over, reminding myself of all the ways I had failed my daughter and my God.

It is so easy for us to believe that we, as trauma mommas, should know better how to respond in any given situation. When we fail to do what we consider good parenting, we berate ourselves and maybe even God telling him that he made a mistake in trusting us with his little ones. It has occurred to me over the last several months that God doesn't need adoptive parents who always know what to do. He needs adoptive parents who are willing to lean into his wisdom and direction, parents who love and keep loving despite the pricks to our hearts.

REFLECTIONS

I'm working on learning that the hurting heart outbursts have nothing to do with who I am or what God has called me to do. Would you join me in praying for the healing of our own hurts, so they don't conflict with our children's pains?

PRAYER:

Loving Father, there are moments in this mothering journey when I feel weary from the heartache. The professionals tell me that my children's behavior is not personal, but I still feel the sting. This is too hard! Thank you for the promise that nothing is too hard for you. Help me find healing in that. Amen.

THE CRIES OF YOUR HEART:

_____

_____

_____

_____

_____

_____

_____

_____

WE NEED AN INTERPRETER

*You have revealed the paths of life to me; you will fill
me with gladness in your presence.*
–Acts 2:28

INITIALLY, our middle daughter struggled most
with the idea of being removed from her family of
origin and relocated to a home of strangers. She
quickly saddled herself with unrealistic expectations
and perfectionism to the extreme. She also developed
a tendency to literally flee from conflict by running
away from home. With each time she left home, the
level of danger she put herself into was greater and
greater.

"What if you take that running and channel it into
something good?" A friend suggested.

Of course! I invited my daughter to come along on
some of my shorter training distances. Fairly soon, it
was apparent that I couldn't run fast enough for her.
So, we signed her up for a cross country track team.
No one would have guessed that she was such a skilled
runner. But she still carried the baggage of
perfectionism.

At one of her final track meets of the season, as
usual, the coach assigned her a time goal. I went off to
cheer for our youngest, who was competing at the
elementary level at the same time as when the middle

school heat took off. I didn't see my middle daughter again until she was already across the finish line.

It was customary for us to meet up at the finish line, where I would grab my daughter in a hug and spin around in a circle. But this time, when our eyes met, she looked ill. Rushing to her side, I noticed the tears I had not seen from a distance.

"Sweet Cheeks, what's wrong?"

She collapsed into me, allowing the sobs to finally come. "I, I, I didn't make my t, t, time!"

I understood immediately from that brief, tearful exchange that *My daughter believed that she had failed.* was not spoken. My daughter believed that she had failed. This precious, sweet, thoughtful eleven-year-old had failed herself, me, the coach, the team, the world.

Team members came to encourage her. They told her she ran a good race, that the course was slippery from mud and almost nobody made their time. There was no consoling her. The coach came into view, and the tears flowed freely.

"What if Coach won't let me be on the team anymore?"

Oh, the fear and heartache in that question. My girl found something that transformed her angst. It had helped her with all of what we call "the feels."

So, I reached out and gripped the coach's arm. Pulling him over, I said, "This sweet girl is worried that you won't let her stay on the team because she didn't make her time."

Giving a grandfatherly smile, he said, "No one made their time because I messed up and gave you the wrong times." Finally, there was some relief, and she could breathe again.

Isn't it interesting how several people can use similar words to bring you relief and comfort, but until you hear it from the person who counts, you aren't able to receive it? When I think of a situation where we can all relate to the struggle, I am reminded that kids from painful pasts feel the struggle times a thousand because their "feeling foundation" is built on fear. The more our family grows relationally and spiritually, the more I see how important it is to invite each member to look to the Comforter in every moment of life.

REFLECTIONS

Do you wish to soothe your children's hurting hearts? Pray with me that, as mommas of kids who hurt, we will become more and more in tune with God's voice.

PRAYER:

Lord, teach me through your Spirit—the great comforter—how to lead my children onto a path of seeking you to interpret and soothe the hurts that they cannot name nor comprehend. Amen.

THE CRIES OF YOUR HEART:

_____

_____

_____

_____

_____

_____

_____

_____

WHEN WORDS FAIL TO COME

But when you pray, go into your private room, shut your door, and pray to your Father who is in secret. And your Father who sees in secret, will reward you.
– Matthew 6:6

"DEAR MRS. NAGEL, I'm writing to you regarding your son and his apparent struggles with his Science assignments. He has been asking other students for the answers on his assignments during Study Hall. Is it possible for you to find the time to assist him and encourage him to do his work at home?"

Hmmm...that was an interesting turn of events. According to my son, just two days prior, he liked Science, and yes, he liked his Science teacher, and no, he didn't need my help in any of his classes. As I drove to pick up my kids from school that day, my puzzlement morphed into frustrated and then angry prayers.

> *What am I doing wrong, Lord? Please show me what to do.*

"Lord, why? Can't I have one day that doesn't turn into a battle? I'm so tired, Lord. Don't you see it? Don't you care? I can't spend the rest of my life battling these children. What am I doing wrong, Lord? Please show me what to do."

Then I put on a happy face and greeted each child as they climbed into the van. We chattered away about the happenings of the day, expectations for the rest of the day, and of course, a brief discussion about our dinner plans. Before joining our family, my kids had lived with much uncertainty about when they would eat next; and now they needed to know there was a plan. So, any talks about Science homework would have to wait!

My head hurt just thinking about it. I don't like being lied to. My kids know that there is not much I hate more than lying. My evening was plagued with simmering thoughts of frustration, anger, and disappointment.

Against my better judgment, I started the conversation with my son from a position of irritation. "I got an email from your Science teacher today." No response. "Do you want to guess what it was about?" Silence. "From what I understand, she believes you are asking other kids for their answers because you haven't bothered to do it yourself. Is that about right?" Slight nod. Ramrod spine. Tight jaw.

"I need you to help me understand what's the problem." My anger had seeped into my tone. "You can't continue to copy off the other kids. You must learn this stuff."

Tears were building in his eyes. Then, finally, "It's too hard!" Through pauses between sobs, nose-blowing, and trying to catch his breath, my son conveyed a story of feeling lost and confused during most of his Science class.

"Why didn't you ask me for help?" My tone was softening.

"Because I didn't think you would know." BAM! There was an underlying dilemma. I'm an educated woman; my son was fully aware of my education and knowledge from those prior years when we had homeschooled. Yet fear of failure, of disappointing or being rejected by me, and who knows what else was crippling my very intelligent boy from feeling secure enough to ask for my help.

REFLECTIONS

When life doesn't turn out to be as smooth as we hoped because our kids aren't cooperating with us, it's time to stop and pray. We don't need to pray in some perfectly outlined biblical order. Instead, what is required is being honest with the one who made us. "This is hard. I'm feeling frustrated. Help me." God knows our hearts, and when they cry out, he already knows the answer.

208

PRAYER:

Father, sometimes I worry that my prayers are not adequate for you to take notice. In those times, I pray less and worry more. Help me remember that it is not merely eloquent prayers that you desire. Your Holy Spirit delivers, to you, the cries of my heart for my children with no need for spoken words. Amen.

THE CRIES OF YOUR HEART:

_____

_____

_____

_____

_____

_____

_____

STUCK ON THE SPIN CYCLE

God, hear my cry; pay attention to my prayer. I call to
you from the ends of the earth when my heart is
without strength. Lead me to a rock that
is high above me.
—Psalm 61:1-2

TEARS BURNED my eyes and blurred my vision as
they spilled onto my red-hot cheeks. It was a test, a
test I didn't have to take again. The choice was mine
all along, just like the last test and the one before that.

Still, taking the bait, I believed I could somehow
eventually succeed in proving my love for my kids. But
I was wrong. My daughter sat there sobbing, wiping
tears from her cheeks as she gave me that look. You
know, the expression that says, "You are the cruelest,
most awful mom on the planet. I'd be better off living
with the chickens."

I hated myself. These kids came from unimaginable
trauma. How could I let myself get angry enough to
yell—again?! Taking a deep breath, I invited my
daughter to join me. "You need to calm yourself. Let's
breathe. Three counts in. You are safe. Three counts
out. Again. Three counts in. No one is leaving you.
Three counts out."

It was a fight to hold back my own tears. With my
jaw tight, and voice soft, I continued, "Three counts in.
You are loved by me. Three counts out. You are loved

by Dad. Try not to swallow the sobs. Three counts in. You are loved by God. Three counts out."

Finally, her breathing calmed, and her tears subsided. It didn't have to go that way. We were supposed to be having fun making birthday cards for a neighbor. How is it that family fun almost always managed to turn into a family fight? Why? Why can't I get this right? Why can't I keep these darn tears under control?

Swallowing past the gravel in my throat and begging my tears to retreat, I spoke softly, "Sweetheart, there is nothing you can do to make me not love you. There is nothing you can do to make me send you away. There is nothing you can do to get rid of me. You are my daughter. God gave you to me, and he doesn't make mistakes."

> *God gave you to me, and he doesn't make mistakes.*

With that said, I turned and carefully climbed the stairs to my bedroom, my retreat, then collapsed on the bed. Now the tears flowed unrestrained as I choked on my sobs. "How did we get here again, Lord? Forgive me for being such an awful parent. I'm sorry you trusted these kids to me, and I'm completely screwing them up."

Before falling into a fitful sleep, I breathed, "God, please help me get this right."

Hopelessness and helplessness both manage to work their way into our minds as adoptive mommas.

We want so badly for our children to heal from their troubles, that we often forget we are the mentor, not the master. God knows their past, and he understands ours, as well.

REFLECTIONS

Most importantly, God has seen the future, and he's already there. Why not join me in asking the Lord for the grace we need to trust him to live out his plan through us rather than trusting our own flawed ability.

PRAYER:

When my family cycles for several consecutive difficult days, it feels like we are moving backward instead of forward. And when it feels like the pendulum is going to fly off into oblivion, remind me, Lord, that you called me to this beautiful family arrangement, and that you promised to live it through me. Amen.

THE CRIES OF YOUR HEART:

_____

_____

_____

_____

_____

_____

_____

_____

WHERE CAN I GET A MAP?

Therefore, strengthen your tired hands and weakened knees, and make straight paths for your feet, so that what is lame may not be dislocated but healed instead.
−Hebrews 12:12

WE WERE in the midst of the season, typically referred to as the "cold and flu season." The familiar and comforting aroma of homemade chicken soup filled the house. Reflecting on the blessed experience of observing my mother nurse her five children back to health, I counted out vitamins, poured orange juice, and occasionally stirred the soup. It felt good to nurture my family through this time.

An unfamiliar sound disrupted my reverie like a bump in the night−a sound you know you heard before but can't identify. Pausing to listen, I heard it again. It was muffled.

Stepping into the family room, I spotted my son curled up on the couch, jaw clenched, eyes wide, and face red. "Are you okay in here?" He nodded. "It seems like something is wrong. Are you sure you are okay?"

It felt good to nurture my family through this time.

Another nod. Then the mystery sound. A cough. It wasn't an ordinary cough, though. My precious newly adopted eight-year-old was fighting with all his strength to keep his coughing from escaping his mouth!

It was painful to watch as his chest heaved instinctively, and he tightened his jaw even more. His fearful eyes shot straight to mine as if willing me to dismiss an infraction.

"Buddy, are you trying to not cough?" He gave a slow and cautious nod. Then another stifled cough shook his small body. "You are allowed to cough, son. God gave our bodies the ability to cough and sneeze as a way to try and get the bad stuff out."

He turned his face and coughed into a pillow, still not convinced. Moving closer, I sat beside him and coughed deliberately into the bend in my elbow. His uncertain eyes stayed on me. I coughed again, harder. Then I imitated his stifled version of a cough. What followed was an exercise is learning how to cough and a more detailed lesson on the purpose of coughing.

"Weren't you allowed to cough before?" He looked down but didn't respond. It didn't matter. He didn't need to respond; I already knew.

When parenting kids who have begun their lives under high stress and uncertainty, it is impossible to anticipate everything they need to learn. While it is true that if we didn't teach them, they probably don't know, our task is uncharted. There is no checklist of items to cover before a child reaches a certain age. We must take on the lessons as they come, always on alert for teaching moments. It's exhausting.

When you notice something "too late," it's easy to believe you have failed your kids...again.

REFLECTIONS

Let's not forget that we have the most excellent example of a parent from God himself. He's not asking us to get it perfect. He's asking us to use his word and truth as a kind of road map that leads our kids and us into his perfect rest. Will you join me in praying for his guidance?

PRAYER:

I need your strength and direction as I walk the uncharted path of parenting kids from hard places, God. Teach me to keep my eyes on you so that the enemy cannot distract or discourage me from resting in your healing ability. Amen.

THE CRIES OF YOUR HEART:

_____

_____

_____

_____

_____

_____

_____

_____

LET IT SHINE

*That light shines in the darkness, and yet the darkness
did not overcome it.*
− John 1:5

SALLY SAT on the ledge of the window, keeping a
watchful eye on her brothers and sister below. They
played and wrestled, seemingly unaware of potential
dangers. She had been welcomed to join in the fun, but
her fear of danger was too intense. She startled at
each unexpected noise, and her eyes grew wider
straining to take in as much as possible. The others
continued in their excitement over the fresh grass,
and tasty herbs planted just for them.

The sidewalk, warm from the sun, encouraged them
to lounge contentedly, with their bellies full, and
satisfied. No one seemed to notice Sally's absence as
they basked in the glory of a summer day. That is until
a pair of turkey vultures floated into view.
Synchronized in their flight, they moved as one across
the open sky, always scanning the ground for a feast.
It was their lunchtime or their second breakfast; you
can never tell with vultures.

I clapped my hands together loudly at the sight of
them, and sang out, "Kitties in the house, kitties in the
house. Hurry! Hurry! Kitties in the house." Reluctantly,
three black critters scurried inside. Sally met them at

the bottom of the staircase, sniffing, inspecting, even meowing a reprimand about vultures.

When my daughter first suggested a story about Sally, I assumed it was because Sally will have no part of any human contact aside from my daughter. Sally primarily lives in my middle girl's bedroom, coming out mostly for a snack and a litter box break. My animal-loving girl soaks up all the love and snuggles Miss Sally has to offer.

But my sweet daughter had made a remarkable connection. She said, "I've been thinking about how Sally is like some people. We are all invited to trust God, but some of us are so afraid we just sit behind the glass and watch everyone else have fun. We feel left out because we decide not to do it." What an appropriate analogy. I swear my kids are all going to be preachers one day!

It also occurs to me how much Sally represents kids from hard beginnings. Even though she came to us as a kitten more than three years ago, she is still as terrified and skittish as the day she was caught up in the rescuer's trap. A knock on the front door, a loud sneeze down the hallway, an adult entering the room all send Sally to the underbelly of the bed where she has created for herself a hole. There is no convincing her that she is safe.

> *I swear my kids are all going to be preachers one day!*

Sometimes as adoptive mommas, we think it's possible to put a specific time frame on a traumatized child's ability to move forward into the future rather than backward into the pain. We might say, "They have lived with us longer than they have lived with any other family. That's enough time to get over it." Not true, my sisters.

REFLECTIONS

Trauma or no trauma, we all have dark moments from our past that creep forward and try to define us. It is time to stop looking at our watches and start turning our children's eyes toward the Father of light.

PRAYER:

Lord, some days feel powerfully dark. Shine your light on me, in me, and through me, onto the children you have entrusted to me. Amen.

THE CRIES OF YOUR HEART:

_____

_____

_____

_____

_____

_____

_____

_____

NEW DAY, NEW EVERYTHING

Because of the Lord's faithful love, we do not perish, for His mercies never end. They are new every morning; great is your faithfulness!
−Lamentations 3:22-23

ON MOST MORNINGS in the Nagel household, you can find me in the kitchen wearing my favorite blue robe and some fuzzy slippers. Before anyone else is awake for the day, I like to have a few moments of some proper stretching, maybe a three- or four-mile run, a sit down with the Lord and his Word, and at least one cup of coffee. I would like to tell you that my morning routine always makes for a perfect start to any given day, but I would not be telling the truth.

Some mornings I am just plain crabby. There are mornings where the only thing that happens before everyone else gets up is gulping down a giant cup of coffee. And there are still others when I'm stinging from hurtful words or behaviors displayed from one of my kids on the night before. Sometimes I wish I could crawl back into bed and hide−the minute my feet touch the floor.

I love my children. You know, I do. And I always will.

The struggle for me is that they shake things off, moving on much more quickly than I am able. Perhaps one of them has gone to bed the night before, making it abundantly clear that he or she would prefer to be with their bio mom. Or a child may have looked me straight in the eyes and told a lie without the slightest flinch.

But my kids always find recovery and renewal after a good night of sleep. As each child enters the kitchen, they jump right into stories about a silly dream, ask questions about the schedule for the day, or initiate a discussion about what to eat for breakfast. They're hugging on me, standing close, offering to help cook. They have moved on, and I have the challenging task of swallowing my hurt and figuring out how to move on along with them.

> ...staying stuck on the hurt of someone's wrongdoing allows their behavior toward me to be my identity.

It's difficult! And honestly, I don't always want to. Sometimes I prefer that the guilty party feel badly enough to apologize. I want the hug to mean, "I'm so sorry I said you aren't my mom." Just...sometimes...

It occurred to me that staying stuck on the hurt of someone's wrongdoing allows their behavior toward me to be my identity. Instead of being a child of the King who gives me all I need, I allow myself to be a punching bag to children who are deeply hurting and who don't understand why.

REFLECTIONS

I'm so grateful that even on the hard mornings, the sun still comes up, my children are still mine, and God has not turned away from us. Who are you? If you don't know, ask God to show you.

PRAYER:

Merciful God, I can get so wounded by hurtful actions that I allow the enemy to convince me that I'm failing badly. But you give us new mercies every morning. Teach me to extend that mercy toward my family by letting go of yesterday and allowing you to work through me today. Amen.

THE CRIES OF YOUR HEART:

_____

_____

_____

_____

_____

_____

_____

_____

_____

THE ULTIMATE STRENGTH TRAINING PLAN

I have been crucified with Christ, and I no longer live, but Christ lives in me. The life I now live in the body, I live by faith in the Son of God, who loved me and gave himself for me.
—Galatians 2:20

EARLY IN MY LIFE, you would never have found "working out at the gym" on my list of things to do before I die. Then, in my early forties, I realized that better health would result in a better ability to parent well. And so, I took up running. Immediately hooked, and personally being a nerd, I absorbed information about running from every book, magazine, and blog available.

> *She was a runner with lots of insight about listening to your body rather than books...*

There were so many ideas about nutrition, cross-training, minutes versus miles, and setting goals. The information was overwhelming to the point where I questioned every step my running shoes took! Running was no longer fun or refreshing.

One afternoon, while sitting in my son's jiu-jitsu class, I started a conversation with another mom. Turns out, she was a runner with lots of insight about listening to your *body* rather than *books* for the best training plan. She also invited me to join her for a weekly strength and conditioning class.

Deciding it couldn't hurt to try, I attended a class with her. It is still unbelievable all I was able to accomplish in that class, mainly because I was the clumsy girl in high school gym class. The leader had us sweating, breathing heavily, getting up, squatting down, and laughing at our mistakes.

When the class ended, I felt energized and promised to attend the next week. My friend and I left class in a dither of chatter until it came time to walk down the stairs we had so easily ascended an hour earlier. OUCH! That hurt.

"I think I'll just live right here in the stairwell for a while. Come get me when I can move again," I moaned.

She said I couldn't live there, and she made me go home. Some friend she was!

For several days it hurt to go up the stairs to my bedroom. It hurt to sit on the hard dining room chair. But I went to class the following week, participated, survived, and left energized (and sore).

Something happened in my running too. My legs weren't as easily tired out. My lung capacity seemed to double. And my core felt more stable. Running was fun again!

There is no practice gym for preparing to be a therapeutic parent. You must jump in, feet first—and you can't see all the way to the bottom. It's scary, tiring, overwhelming, slow, repetitive, unpredictable, case-specific, isolating, and lonely. Admittedly, some days when I wake up, I want to close my eyes and pretend I'm not alive. Some days I wake up grumpy, and the last thing I want to do is be kind to anyone. There are even days when I wake up and pray, "God, the only way I'm getting out of this bed is if you propel me forward."

REFLECTIONS

It's all okay, reasonable, and understandable to feel like you can't go on. Is it time you offer your physical, mental, and emotional conditioning to the Lord? Rest assured that He is near and is ready to give you all that you need for the day. You can trust him.

PRAYER:

Lord God, it can be so tiring to be a full-time therapeutic parent. It seems like all I do is fail. Remind me that you never intended for me to parent with my own strength and knowledge. You always planned to not only live in me but through me. Teach me to lean into you every moment and to plug into you as my source of life and strength. Amen.

THE CRIES OF YOUR HEART:

_____

_____

_____

_____

_____

_____

_____

_____

WHO'S IN CHARGE AROUND HERE?

He is before all things, and by him
all things hold together.
−Colossians 1:17

"I WANT Grandma!" She wailed in reference to her foster mother.

"Grandma is not here," I replied as she tried to squirm out of my arms.

Then she asked for her brother. When that didn't work, she asked for her sister. Eventually, we were back to, "I want Grandma!"

Exasperated and needing a nap as much as she did, I said, "Grandma is not in charge here. Mom is in charge."

More wailing. More squirming. Then she shouted, "Grandma is the boss!"

On we went through the list of names again, only this time adding her own name in a last-ditch effort to try and win the battle. It had been a long day for us. Our older two children had already climbed on the bus for school.

So, I told her we were going on an adventure, and we ran errands together. I never knew until that day how much more exhausting errands are when you're accompanied by an overly hot and tired three-year-old. Now that I had carried her sweaty, wiggling body into her room, I allowed her to squirm away. She slid to the floor in an epic fit of screaming, kicking, and crying. I stood silent, panting from exertion, and wondered what would happen next.

Within a short time, the kicking stopped. She opened her eyes to see if I was still in the room, let out a few more half-hearted wails, and fell into a deep sleep. I went and collapsed onto my own bed and cried myself to sleep while muttering prayers of apology to the Lord for doing such a poor job with our children.

Our littlest miss had turned three less than a month before our kids came to our home. For a while, she was the most resistant of the three in allowing me to be her mom. In those early months, while we learned to live together as a family, I lost track of who I truly was—her mother.

So, when the tantrums came, oh boy, did they come! And I allowed my inner self to boil up with anxiety. I held onto the belief that every hard moment with my kids meant I was getting motherhood all wrong.

I held onto the belief that every hard moment with my kids meant I was getting motherhood all wrong.

REFLECTIONS

Have you been in a similar place? Do you allow bad moments and hard days to define your identity as a person? As a mother? Your identity is only found in the one who created you—the one who knew you before the world knew you.

PRAYER:

Father, help me remember that I am the manager and not the master. You entrusted your wounded and hurting children to me, not because you expect me to make them into perfect people, but to show them how to represent your loving kindness. Give me the words, thoughts, and actions toward your precious ones that will point them only to you. Amen.

THE CRIES OF YOUR HEART:

_____

_____

_____

_____

_____

_____

_____

_____

TO AN ADOPTED

ON THE DAY that our adoption was made final, we were given an unexpected, yet wonderful gift from the judge who presided over our case. The Honorable Patrick Hillary handed us a copy of the poem below. The verses within both beautifully and succinctly express the gift that is adoption.

The poet's words lend the perfect close to this book; as you read these parting thoughts, be reassured and encouraged by the tremendous opportunity you have been given as an adoptive parent.

I
Did not plant you,
True,
But when
The season is done—
When the alternate
Prayers for sun
And for rain
Are counted—
When the pain
Of weeding
And the pride
Of watching
Are through—

Then
I will hold you
High
A shining sheaf
Above the thousand
Seeds grown wild.

Not my planting,
But by heaven
My harvest—
My own child.

Carol Lynn Pearson

ABOUT THE AUTHOR

TO SAY THAT Beth Nagel is a multi-talented person is an understatement. Wife, mom, teacher, and author are just some of the many hats she wears during any given day. Aside from her creative and inspiring writing, she is a gifted musician and Bible teacher.

Beth is a loving and passionate person who wants to leave the world better than she found it. Using her own life experiences, she wants both biological and adoptive mothers everywhere to know that they are not alone in the struggle to successfully raise their children into adulthood.

Made in the USA
Monee, IL
06 May 2020

29405450R00134